Jesus Christ

Joan and Malcolm Grills

Oxford University Press

4551434

BEDFORDSHIRE
LEISURE
SERVICES
COUNTY COUNCIL

Oxford University Press, Walton Street, Oxford OX2 6DP
Oxford New York Toronto
Delhi Bombay Calcutta Madras Karachi
Petaling Jaya Singapore Hong Kong Tokyo
Nairobi Dar es Salaam Cape Town
Melbourne Auckland

and associated companies in
Beirut Berlin Ibadan Nicosia

Oxford is a trade mark of Oxford University Press

ISBN 0 19 917062 2

Phototypeset by Tradespools Ltd, Frome
Printed in Great Britain by The Alden Press

Contents

Contents

Introduction

a. The Purpose of this book:

This book presents the results of modern Biblical study on a suitable level for use in school. In order to do this we have had to simplify ideas, but we have remained faithful to the conclusions of different scholars. Our starting point has been to examine the Gospels as statements of faith made by Christians of the first century. It is necessary to interpret the Gospels in order for people today, particularly pupils in school, to understand their original meaning. The Gospels are complex documents which cannot be understood by the casual reader. We have tried to reflect the variety of opinion found amongst Biblical scholars, but at the same time, we have presented those conclusions which are generally accepted. In some cases we have also included important alternatives.

b. How to use this book:

The book was written in, and for, the class-room. The style is deliberately concise. Information is given simply so that it may be more easily understood. We have not mentioned details from the Biblical stories unless they required some comment. It is essential that the Bible is used alongside this book. We have used the Revised Standard Version.

We have included material from John's Gospel. Most of this will be found with stories on the same theme from the Synoptic Gospels. The chapter on John's Gospel has information about important passages which have not been discussed elsewhere. We have tried, within the limits of this book, to give some insight into the complexities of John's Gospel.

It is very important that the teacher tells the pupils exactly what is in their particular syllabus. Since this book includes material from all four Gospels some of it will not be required for all examination courses, eg. stories from John's Gospel.

There is a work section at the end of each chapter which is divided into three parts. The first contains comprehension questions which can be answered by using information from the chapter and from the relevant passages in the Bible. The second contains essay questions. The third part is intended to provoke thought. Some of the questions require information found outside the Gospels. Other questions are intended to relate the Gospel stories to modern life and may be useful for group discussion. Further reading has been suggested for both teacher and pupil.

We have attempted to use simple language. An explanation of essential technical words and phrases will be found in the Glossary. Individual stories can be found by consulting the list of Biblical references.

c. The GCSE examinations

Examination questions require detailed knowledge of the Gospel stories. It is insufficient to know only the outline of a story and to invent the rest! It is vital to read the questions carefully and to pay special attention to words such as 'either', or 'or'. It is necessary to distinguish between different types of stories, eg. miracles and parables; nature miracles and healing miracles. It is also important to distinguish between events in the life of Jesus and stories which Jesus told, eg. the meeting with the rich young ruler was an event in Jesus' life and not a parable. (It is thought that even the Gospel writers changed some of the things which Jesus actually said, into things which he did!) This book is a useful aid for examinations because it has been divided into the themes which are needed to answer most examination questions. The work sections provide short answer questions which test understanding and learning. The essay questions are typical of those set in examinations.

The introduction of GCSE means that pupils will be tested by a greater variety of questions. These will include the short answer type found in Section A, the traditional essay question of section B and also the evaluation and interpretation type of question found in section C. The introduction of stimulus material and graded questions into exams means that the higher skills will be tested, rather than just recall of the stories. This book is intended to help students develop these skills.

A priest of the Temple, and the High Priest
wearing the ceremonial robes used only on
the Day of Atonement

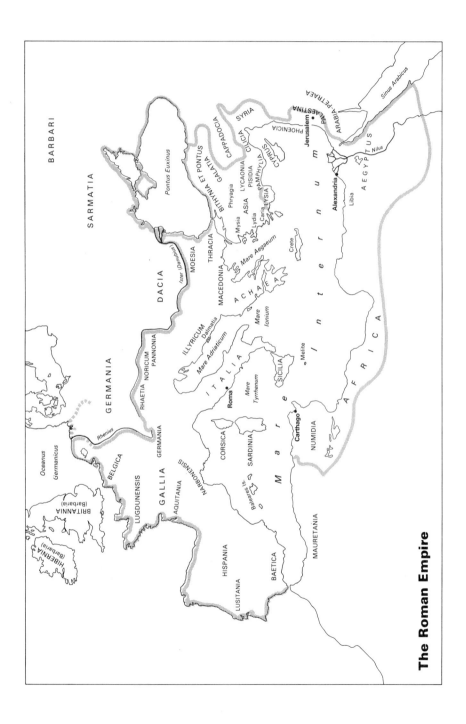

The Roman Empire

The political and religious background

The Gospel writers pass on names, ideas and customs without giving an explanation because their readers were already familiar with them. Though it must be remembered that none of the writers is recording his own experience of Jesus. In order to study the life of Jesus as it is recorded in the Gospels, we must first examine what these unfamiliar terms mean.

1.   The Political Background

'Palestine' is a term used for those areas in and around Israel, under Roman control.

For more than a hundred years before Herod the Great became King, Rome had been involved in the politics of the countries which were on the border of the Roman Empire. In much the same way as today Russia dominates the countries of Eastern Europe, and the U.S.A. seeks to influence the governments of Southern America, Rome backed or opposed rulers and factions.

In 67 B.C. two brothers, Hyrcanus and Aristobulus fought for control of Palestine. Both asked the great Roman General, Pompey, for military aid. Pompey backed Hyrcanus and in 63 B.C. captured Jerusalem. Hyrcanus was an ineffectual ruler and real power was in the hands of his chief minister, Antipater. When civil war broke out in Rome itself, Antipater supported Julius Caesar. Caesar rewarded him by extending the lands ruled by Hyrcanus and giving influential positions to Antipater's sons. Phasael became governor of Jerusalem and Herod, who was only twenty-five years old, became commander of Galilee. Herod showed exceptional ability as a general. After Julius Caesar was assassinated, Herod was nominated as King of Judea in 40 B.C. but he was not able to claim his throne until 37 B.C. In the Roman wars between Anthony and Augustus, Herod supported Anthony but despite this the winner, Augustus, was so impressed with Herod's abilities that he confirmed him as King and eventually extended his realm.

Herod was disliked by many of his subjects for various reasons:

a. He was not a member of the royal family and many regarded him as an upstart.

b. He was only a half Jew and refused to take Judaism seriously except when it was politically necessary. After being appointed King in Rome he offered a sacrifice to Jupiter. He rebuilt the Temple in Jerusalem but he put a huge imperial Eagle over the main gate, which horrified many Jews because they were forbidden to have graven images. He built temples to Augustus in Sebaste, the capital of Samaria, and also in Caesarea.

c. He lived and built, as far as possible in the Greek style, and owed his authority and allegiance to Rome.

d. He had a reputation for great cruelty. A contemporary said that it was safer to be Herod's sow than his son. He made his seventeen year old brother-in-law High Priest and then had him 'accidentally' drowned in the swimming pool of his palace in Jericho. He had his wife and her father, the ex-King Hyrcanus, executed. His two sons and heirs were also executed. When his army criticised his actions he had three hundred of his soldiers beaten to death. Five days before the death of Herod his son, Antipater, who had been confident of succeeding him, was strangled.

e. He interfered in religious matters. He reduced the power of the Sanhedrin and executed fifty-five of its seventy-one members. Both Herod and the Romans nominated and sacked (or executed) High Priests as they saw fit. Between 37 B.C. and 70 A.D. there were twenty-eight High Priests.

However, despite his faults, Herod's reign brought peace and prosperity. After the death of Herod the Great in 4 B.C. the Jews asked the Emperor Augustus to end Herodian rule but the Emperor followed the wishes of Herod the Great by dividing the country between three of his remaining sons: Herod Archelaus was given Judea and Samaria. Philip was given the land to the north east of the Jordan and Herod Antipas was given Galilee, and the land to the east of the Jordan. Therefore, after Herod's death, Galilee, Samaria, Judea, Idumea, and Decapolis were virtually separate states with separate administrations and rulers; but they were all subject to Rome and existed under the watchful eye of the Roman governor of Syria and his legions. Archelaus was deposed in 6 A.D. because of his brutality and incompetence. He was replaced by a Roman Procurator who lived at Caesarea and was responsible for levying taxes and administering justice. Concessions were made to the Jews by the Romans including the exclusion of Roman military standards from Jerusalem because they were regarded as graven images. The Sanhedrin was allowed to retain its power only over religious matters. However, despite these concessions, anti-Roman feeling in Judea was strong. There were often outbreaks of violence against the Romans. In 66 A.D. a series of rebellions

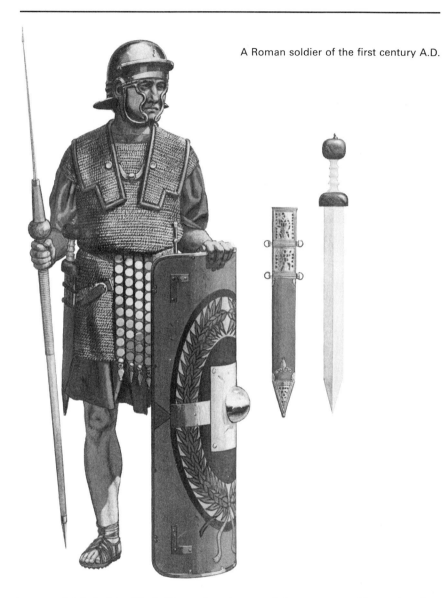

A Roman soldier of the first century A.D.

began which led in 70 A.D. to the siege and destruction of Jerusalem by the Romans.

2.   The Jewish law

The term 'law' in the Gospels usually refers to the Torah, which is composed of the first five books of the Old Testament. The Jews believed that these were given by God to Moses. In the Covenant made at Mt.

15

Sinai the Jews promised to obey the law and God adopted them as his people. However, the law had to be interpreted so that it could be applied to everyday life. This interpretation was made by scholars and teachers and came to be known as the Oral Tradition. eg. the Law said 'The seventh day is the sabbath of the Lord your God; that day you shall not do any work.' (Exodus 20:10). The scholars had to decide what was meant by 'work'. They spent most of their time relating the law to everyday life, legal disputes, and moral issues, but some of them were even prepared to discuss such questions as whether it was 'work' to keep food hot on a fire, or to rescue an animal from a ditch, or even to eat an egg which had been laid on the Sabbath! The Oral law was not kept by all Jews. By the end of the second century A.D. some of it had been written down in the Mishnah.

3.   The importance of the synagogue

Every town and village in Palestine had at least one synagogue. Services were held on the Sabbath and on other days. These were not led by Priests but by elders who were also responsible for the organisation of services. Any male Jew could be invited to give the sermon. According to the Gospels, Jesus was asked to do this on several occasions, eg. Mark 1:21–28; Mk. 6:1–6. There was a paid official who looked after the school which was attached to the synagogue. By the end of the first century A.D. the Jews had developed a widespread system of education. Synagogue services included prayers, and readings from the Torah, in Hebrew, and a sermon or seminar in the native tongue—Aramaic.

4.   The importance of the Temple

Many scholars have put forward the theory that by the time of Jesus the synagogue was more important than the Temple. However the Temple was still very important because it was the only place where sacrifices could be offered. It was thought to be the throne room of God. Herod the Great began to rebuild the Temple on a magnificent scale on the site of the original Temple of Solomon which had been destroyed when the Jews were taken captive to Babylon. He had to flatten the existing Temple buildings to do so. There were four enclosed courts. The outer one was the Court of the Gentiles, where Jesus is described as turning over the tables of those who sold animals and birds for sacrifice (Mk 11:15–17). Around the

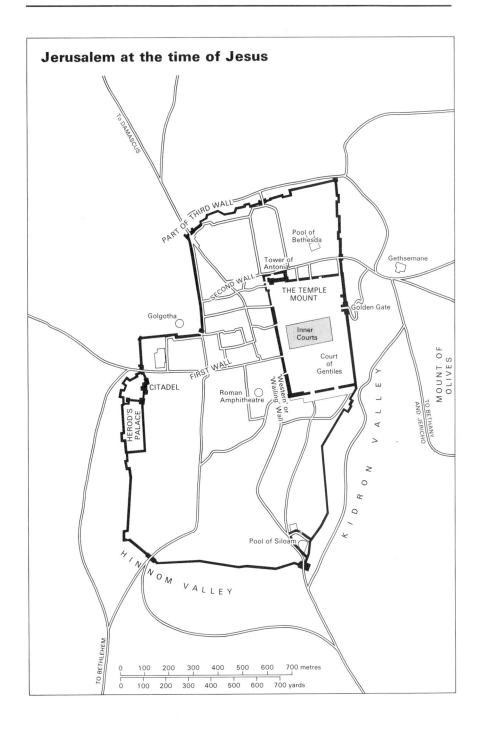

Jerusalem at the time of Jesus

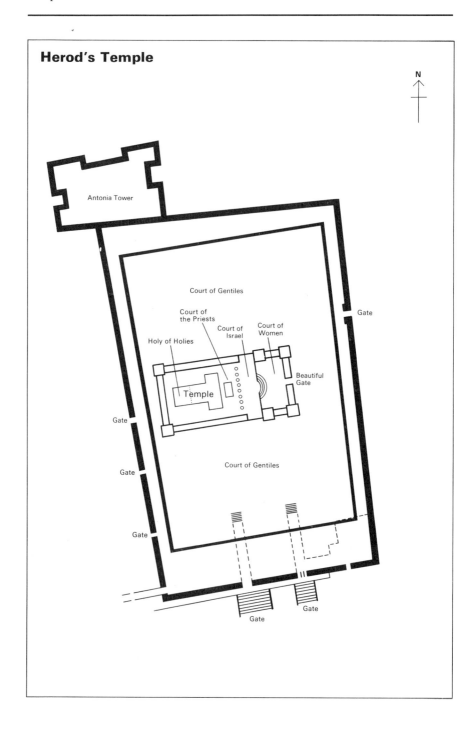

Herod's Temple

N

Antonia Tower

Court of Gentiles

Court of
the Priests

Court of
Israel

Court of
Women

Holy of Holies

Temple

Gate

Beautiful
Gate

Gate

Gate

Gate

Court of Gentiles

Gate

Gate

Court of the Gentiles were covered walks where the scribes taught. This was probably where Luke set the story of Jesus' visit to Jerusalem at the age of twelve, (Lk 2:41–50). The inner courts were the Court of Women, the Court of the men of Israel and the Court of the Priests. At the centre was the Holy of Holies which only the High Priest could enter once a year on the Day of Atonement.

5.   Groups within Judaism

It is important to remember that the Gospels were written for people living in the Roman world. It seems strange and unfortunate that the enemies of Jesus should be seen as 'the Jews' when Jesus, the disciples, and Paul were also Jews. It also seems strange that the Pharisees, Sadducees and Scribes are seen as the villains of the piece when we know from the Gospels and other sources that many of the Pharisees were held in high regard by both the people and Jesus himself. Some of Jesus' teaching is close to the teaching of many of the Pharisees. Paul, a Pharisee himself, was educated by the Pharisee, Gamaliel, who defended Peter and John before the Sanhedrin. (Acts 5: 33–42)

The Gospels were written during or after the great Jewish revolt. In order to make Jesus' teaching more acceptable to the Roman world it would have been necessary to play down his Jewish background. After the destruction of the Temple in 70 A.D. the leading Pharisee, Johannan ben Zakkai, got permission from the Romans to establish an 'academy' at Javneh on the coast. Here the remaining scribes and scholars gathered and soon assumed the spiritual leadership of the Jewish people. Their first object was the survival of Judaism. The Christian interpretation of the law, their attitude to gentiles, and their belief in Christ's authority above that of the Torah inevitably caused a rift between Jewish Christians and Jews. But it would be wrong to suppose that all Pharisees were the implacable enemies of Jesus.

a Pharisees

The name probably means 'separate ones'. They may have lived together in close communities in particular areas of towns and cities but they were not separated from ordinary people by their strict observance of the ritual law. They were a much respected group in the Jewish community. A man who wished to become a Pharisee had to agree to keep the ritual law before he was accepted. Pharisees often attended the three daily hours of prayer and fasted twice a week. They were not priests. They usually belonged to the middle classes. They held influential positions and had a good deal of political influence at times when rulers sympathetic to their aims were in power. They were tolerated by the ruling authorities because they were supported by the people, eg. when they refused to take the oath of obedience to Caesar, Herod merely fined them, whereas other people were put to death. They differed from the Sadducees on three main points:

i) They observed the Oral Tradition and accepted the Prophets and the Writings as well as the Torah.

ii) They believed in the survival of the soul after death.

iii) They believed that God controlled people's lives.

b Sadducees

Josephus says that Sadducees were aristocratic, priestly families who took their name from Zadok who was a High Priest at the time of Solomon. However it is possible that their name is derived from the Greek word 'Syndics'. These were civic officials who were responsible for legal advice. If this is so then the Sadducees in the Gospels would have been a small, select group of influential, wealthy men who had great power. They opposed any ideas which threatened the status quo, eg. the expectation of the Messiah. They differed from the Pharisees on three main points:

i) They accepted the Torah but rejected the Oral Tradition, Prophets and Writings.

ii) They did not believe in the survival of the soul after death.

iii) They did not believe that God concerned himself with everyday matters, and taught that men must solve their own problems with the aid of the Torah.

c Scribes

A Jew could usually become a Scribe at the age of forty after many years of study. Scribes could make decisions about Jewish ritual and law, act as judges at criminal proceedings and pass judgement in civil cases. They were called 'Rabbi' and people rose respectfully as they passed by. Jesus himself is often addressed as 'Rabbi' in the Gospels. They were given the most important places at feasts and in the synagogues. They were especially revered because they interpreted the Oral Tradition for ordinary people. The Jews regarded them as the inheritors of the prophetic tradition. The most important Pharisees were also Scribes.

d Herodians

Little is known about this group. They were supporters of the Herod family, especially Herod Antipas, and not a religious sect. Some of them believed, for a time, that Herod the Great was the Messiah!

e The Zealots

According to Josephus, the Zealot movement began in A.D. 6 when the poll tax was introduced. They believed that since 'God was their only ruler and King', they had to oppose Roman interference in Jewish affairs. They used violence and assasinations. The Zealots led the rebellion against Rome in A.D. 66. The war ended in A.D. 73 when the fortress at Masada was beseiged by the Romans. Josephus records that the Zealots who occupied the fortress killed themselves and their families rather than be captured by the Romans. According to Luke one of Jesus' disciples was called Simon the Zealot. (6:15) There are hints in the Gospels that some Zealots may have hoped that Jesus would lead a rebellion. It is probable that Barabbas was a Zealot.

f The Essenes

Essenes lived in closed communities, usually in desolate places. Jews could only be admitted to the community after three years of study. Ritual bathing in a 'mikve' was an important part of their life. They swore to revere God, to be faithful to their comrades, not to tell their doctrines to others and to preserve the books of the sect and the names of the angels. Some sources say that they were celibate others say that they were married. They wore white clothes and prayed at sunrise. Men who were convicted of major offences were expelled from the order. The Dead Sea Scrolls, which were discovered in 1947 at Qumran, have led many scholars to conclude that the Qumran community were Essenes.

N.B. Further information about the Essenes will be found in Chapter Four.

6.   Despised Groups

Occupations which tempted people to be dishonest or to break the ritual law were despised by some pious Jews.

eg. Shepherds were regarded as dishonest by extremists because they led their flocks onto other people's land. But it must be remembered that Abraham, David and most of the founders of Judaism had been shepherds.

Butchers were tempted to sell meat from imperfect animals.

Shopkeepers were tempted to cheat their customers.

Even doctors were tempted to attend the rich and neglect the poor and came in for criticism from the extremists. They also became ritually unclean when they touched blood and dead bodies.

a Tax collectors

The title 'tax-collectors' is used in the Gospels when a better translation would be 'publican'. Publicans paid the Romans for the privilege of collecting public taxes in a particular area. They divided this area into smaller sections and sold permission to collect taxes. The tax-collectors mentioned in the Gospels were these subordinate officials. The Romans expected a certain amount from each area which was paid by the publican. The people had to pay a much larger amount and the profits were kept by the tax-collectors and publicans. They had a very bad reputation because they were dishonest. They were also hated because they worked for the Romans. Tax collectors could not give money in alms because it was tainted. They were also forbidden to act as witnesses.

b Samaritans

After the death of Solomon the ten northern tribes broke away from the two southern tribes to form a separate kingdom which was called Israel, with Samaria as its capital. Israel was defeated by the Assyrians in 722 B.C. Up to a fifth of the population was exiled and foreigners were introduced into Israel who intermarried with the Jews. The Samaritans were their descendents. The Southern kingdom of Judah was defeated by the Babylonians in 586 B.C. and most of the population was exiled. They did not marry foreigners and when they returned they had maintained their racial purity. They began to rebuild the Temple in Jerusalem. The Samaritans offered to help but they were refused. The Samaritans then built their own Temple on Mount Gerizim. This was destroyed by the Jews under John Hyrcannus in 108 B.C. and rebuilt. Sacrifices are held there to this day.

It is possible that at the end of the first century B.C. there was a temporary relaxation in the hatred. Herod married a Samaritan woman which could have been an attempt to join the two communities. During Herod's reign Samaritans may have been allowed to enter the inner court of the Temple. However, in 6–9 B.C., some Samaritans desecrated the Temple by throwing human bones into the Sanctuary during the Passover and the intense hatred was therefore renewed. The evidence of the Gospels and Josephus is of total hostility between Jews and Samaritans. It was dangerous for Jews from Galilee to pass through Samaria on their way to Jerusalem. Samaritans also served as auxiliaries in its Roman army. The Samaritans kept the Jewish law but the Jews regarded them as an idolatrous cult because they believed that Mt. Gerizim was a holy mountain. It is against this background that we can appreciate Jesus' attitude to Samaritans.

7.   The place of women

A woman had to cover her face in public. A man was forbidden to be alone with a woman or to look lustfully at a married woman. There was a Rabbinic proverb 'Do not gossip much with a woman' which was applied by some to their own wives! It was regarded as preferable that a woman, especially an unmarried woman, should not go out at all. This strict seclusion was not possible in poor families where the woman had to work. Women had more freedom in rural areas. They went to the well and worked in the fields. A girl was only educated in skills such as needlework, weaving and cooking. Up to the age of twelve and a half her father had complete power over her. At marriage she came under the authority of her husband, who was obliged to support her. In return, the woman had to fulfil household duties. Girls were usually married by the age of thirteen. Under Jewish Law a woman could not divorce her husband unless he followed a despised trade such as dung collecting or beat her, or refused to have sexual intercourse with her.

The Gospels, especially Luke, contain many stories about Jesus meeting women, eg. Martha and Mary (Lk 10:38–42) and women were amongst his followers (Mk 15:40–41). Some Jews sought to isolate women because they believed that sexual desire could not be controlled. Jesus, however, expects his followers to be pure. (Mt 5:28)

8.   The Kingdom of God

N.B. The terms 'Kingdom of God' and 'Kingdom of Heaven' have the same meaning. The Jews used 'heaven' to show respect for God by not using his name.

The Jews understood the phrase 'Kingdom of God' to refer to the power and authority of God and not to an area of land which God ruled over. They thought that the Kingdom was both in the present and in the future:

    a. in the present, God guided the Jewish people.

    b. in the future, God would be accepted by the whole world.

The Kingdom of God is the main theme of Jesus' teaching. Mark (1:15) summarizes Jesus' message as 'The time is fulfilled and the Kingdom of God is at hand; repent, and believe in the Gospel.' God's reign is so near that the signs of God's power could be seen in the miracles of Jesus. There has been much discussion about whether Jesus spoke of the Kingdom of God as a present or a future event. There are references to both in the Gospels, eg. 'Thy Kingdom come', (Mt 6:10) and '. . . but if it is by the finger of God that I cast out demons, then the Kingdom of God has come upon you.' (Lk 11:20). One leading scholar, C.H. Dodd maintains that Jesus only spoke of the Kingdom as being in the present and that the future references reflect the belief of the early Church. However, another scholar, Joachim Jeremias, thinks that to understand Jesus as saying that the Kingdom of God had already come is a misunderstanding of the Greek which really means that the Kingdom is 'near'. An alternative is to say that Jesus described the Kingdom as being present like a seed which will one day become the harvest. The Kingdom of God is near enough for people to have to make a decision to accept Jesus' teaching. Jesus did not use the idea of the Kingdom to encourage Jewish nationalist hopes for freedom from the Romans. He did not preach about the restoration of the Kingdom of David, but warned about the day of Judgement and the coming of the Son of Man.

Work Section

Section A

1. When did Palestine become part of the Roman Empire?
2. Who was appointed as King of Judea?
3. When did Herod the Great die?
4. How was the Kingdom divided after Herod's death?
5. List two concessions made to the Jews by the Romans.
6. What happened in 66 A.D.?
7. What is the Torah?
8. What is the Oral Tradition?
9. What is the Mishnah?
10. Describe a synagogue service.
11. What was the synagogue used for apart from services?
12. How was the Temple different to the synagogue?
13. List the different courts of the Temple.
14. List the most important points about: **a** Pharisees, **b** Sadducees and **c** Scribes.
15. Who were the Zealots?
16. Describe the life of an Essene.
17. Why were some occupations despised by the Jews?
18. Why were tax collectors especially despised?
19. Explain reasons for the hatred between Jews and Samaritans.
20. Describe the part played by women in Jewish society.
21. Explain what Jesus meant by the phrase 'The Kingdom of God'.
22. Why is it important to understand the meaning of the names and places explained in this chapter?

Section B

23. Describe the political situation in Israel at the time of Jesus. What was the Jewish hope for the future? 10,10.

24. What is the difference between the Torah and the Oral Tradition? Describe the main groups within Judaism. 5,15.

---

25. Describe the attitude of the Jews to **a** tax collectors,
b Samaritans and **c** Women. 6,7,7.

26. What information can be found in the Gospels about worship in
a the synagogue and **b** the Temple? 10,10.

Section C

27. Look up the references to Herod the Great in the index and
assess his character.

28. Which groups might be regarded as the modern equivalents of
the Zealots?

29. Which occupations might be thought to be despised today?

30. Look up references to Samaritans in the index and assess Jesus'
attitude to them.

31. What would a member of the Women's Liberation Movement
think of the attitude to women in Jewish society at the time of
Jesus?

32. Further information will be found in:

The Jewish War, Josephus.
The Dead Sea Scrolls, G. Vermes.
The Jews from Alexander to Herod, D.S. Russell.

Understanding the Gospels

1. Why the Gospels were written

In the years immediately after the Resurrection there was no need to write an account of the life and teaching of Jesus. The disciples witnessed the events and told others, who then believed that Jesus was the Messiah. The early Christians expected the imminent return of Jesus to establish the Kingdom of God on earth. Details of Jesus' life, and his teaching, were formed into stories and sayings which were passed on accurately. However, as Christianity spread throughout the Roman Empire these traditions were adapted to make them relevant to people of different backgrounds. Jewish Christians would have understood more easily the origins of Jesus' teaching and needed a different emphasis from that of Gentile Christians. The speeches found in Acts and John's Gospel are good examples of how the Christian message was adapted to meet the needs of these different groups.

In A.D. 66 Jewish nationalists began an ill-fated rebellion against Roman authority in Palestine. Christians had to flee from Jerusalem. There is a tradition that James, the brother of Jesus, who was the leader of the Church in Jerusalem, was killed by a mob. In Rome, Christians were persecuted when Nero used them as scape-goats after the fire of Rome. According to tradition the two greatest Church leaders, Peter and Paul, were both executed at this time. If the Gospels had not been written then the oral accounts of the life of Jesus would have been so changed that the historical core could have been entirely lost. The word 'Gospel' is taken from the beginning of Mark (1:1). It means 'good news'.

In the first two centuries after the Resurrection many accounts of the life of Jesus and instructional letters were written. The New Testament contains the most reliable Gospels and letters. Matthew, Mark and Luke are called the Synoptic Gospels because they present a similar picture of Jesus. The word 'synoptic' means 'from the same viewpoint'. The Gospels consist of a collection of individual stories (called pericopes) which the authors have linked together. It is thought, however, that the story of the death of Jesus was preserved as one continuous account from an early stage. The Gospels do not give a chronological account of the ministry of

Jesus as we would expect when reading a modern biography. In order to understand the Gospels we have to see them through the eyes of the early Christians for whom they were written.

2. Biblical Criticism

At the time when the Gospels were written people had a different attitude towards history. The Gospel writers believed that Jesus was the Son of God. Their aim was to tell the story of Jesus in such a way as to make this clear to their readers. Biblical scholars have tried to distinguish between the historical core of the Gospels—the actual story of the man Jesus—and the beliefs and traditions which were added to this core. The story of Jesus was passed on by believers to help other people to gain faith. After Jesus died, his followers were inspired by the Spirit to develop his teaching and apply it to their own lives. The Gospels combine this later teaching with Jesus' own teachings.

It was thought that the Synoptic Gospels gave a factual, biographical account of Jesus, but John's Gospel was a theological account, ie. it was more concerned with the significance of Jesus than with the historical events. Today the view is that the Synoptic Gospels are not simple biographies but have a different theology from John. Each writer has his own view of Jesus and expresses this in the Gospel.

3. The Synoptic Problem

The study of the connexion between the first three Gospels is called the Synoptic Problem. It is easy to see that the Gospels are similar but more difficult to explain why. The answer accepted generally is that Mark's Gospel was written first and used by Matthew and Luke as a source of information.

The following evidence supports this view:

  a. Matthew uses 90% of Mark,
     Luke uses 65%

  b. In the sections copied from Mark:
     Matthew uses 51% of Mark's words,
     Luke uses 53%

c. Where all three Gospels have parallel accounts there are example of:

Matthew and Mark agreeing against Luke,
Luke and Mark agreeing against Matthew,
but none of Luke and Matthew agreeing against Mark.

d. Matthew and Luke generally follow Mark's order of events.

e. Matthew and Luke improve Mark's Greek and style of writing.

f. Matthew and Luke present a more idealised view of the disciples than Mark and elaborate his miracle stories.

This explains the similarities between Mark and Luke and Matthew but cannot explain why Luke and Matthew share some stories which are not in Mark. This problem can be solved by the theory that there was a second source, 'Q' which was used only by Matthew and Luke.

THE Q DOCUMENT

There are about two hundred verses which are in both Matthew and Luke but not in Mark. These verses are so similar that it is thought that they may have been taken from a written document. This lost source is called 'Q' from the German word for source 'Quelle'. Q was not a complete life of Jesus but a collection of sayings with some biographical details. It is possible that Q was composed by Christians influenced by John the Baptist because it contains information about John that is not in Mark's Gospel. It probably originated in Antioch in Syria, and may have been written before Mark.

Matthew and Luke use Q in different ways.

a Luke:

uses the material in five blocks. It is possible that originally Luke's Gospel only contained Luke's special material and Q (see below). Where Q and Mark have similar material Luke copies Q.

b Matthew:

Matthew combines Mark and Q when they have similar material. Since Matthew included 90% of Mark it is likely that he also included most of Q.

It is impossible to discover what Q contained. We cannot assume that all of Q has been used by both Matthew and Luke, or that they used the same version. Matthew may have included material from Q that Luke has missed out and vice versa. It is generally assumed that Q was a written document because there is a close similarity between the passages in Matthew and Luke but it may have been a common oral source. The task of trying to reconstruct Q has been compared with attempting to make a pig from a string of sausages!

Some passages thought to belong to Q are:

Luke 3:2–9, 16–17, 21–22
Luke 4:1–16a
Luke 6:20–7:10
Luke 7:18–35
Luke 9:57–60
Luke 10:2–16, 21–24
Luke 11:9–52
Luke 12:1–12, 22–59
Luke 13:18–35
Luke 14:11, 26–27, 34–35
Luke 16:13, 16–18
Luke 17:1–6, 20–37
Luke 19:11–27

These passages are from Luke's Gospel as they are thought to be closer to what was in 'Q' than those found in Matthew.

MATERIAL SPECIAL TO MATTHEW (M)

At one time Matthew's Gospel was thought to have been written by the disciple of that name. However, since the author copied from Mark this is unlikely. The link with Matthew the disciple may be that he collected together sayings of Jesus (logia) and Old Testament prophecies, which were included in the Gospel. Matthew's Gospel shows that Jesus fulfilled these prophecies. He also includes incidents and teaching which belong to the early church rather than to the time of Jesus. Matthew's special source (M) may have been a written or an oral source.

Some examples of M are:

	1:1–2:23	*The birth stories*
	18:25–35	*The parable of the unforgiving servant*
	21:14–16	*Healings in the Temple and the fulfilment of Psalm 8:2*
	25:1–13	*The parable of the wise and foolish girls*
	28:2–4	*The earthquake*

28:11–15   *The bribing of the soldiers*
28:16–20   *The command to baptise*

MATERIAL SPECIAL TO LUKE (L)

Some scholars believe that there was a first edition of Luke's Gospel which contained Luke's special material and Q. This is called 'Proto-Luke', but it would not have been a complete account of the life of Jesus. Luke later inserted Mark's Gospel into the first draft to form the Gospel which we know today. The alternative view is that Luke used Mark and Q together with the oral traditions which he collected.

Some examples of L are:

1:5–2:52	*The birth stories*
3:10–14	*The teaching of John the Baptist*
10:29–37	*The parable of the Good Samaritan*
14:7–14	*Teaching on humility*
15:1–32	*Parables of the lost sheep, lost coin, and Prodigal Son*
19:1–10	*Zacchaeus*

Therefore the similarities and differences between the first three Gospels are explained by: Matthew used Mark, Q, and M,
Luke   used Mark, Q, and L.

4.   The relationship between John and the Synoptic Gospels

See Chapter 13 for a full discussion of John.

John's Gospel is usually thought to have been written after the Synoptic Gospels in about 100–110 A.D., possibly in Ephesus. It could not have been written by John the disciple but it may contain an understanding of

Jesus passed on by John. It is almost certain that the author of John would have known Mark's Gospel and possibly Luke, but he does not follow the order of events found in the Synoptics. It is incorrect to say that John is a 'theological' Gospel and the Synoptics are 'historical', because all the Gospels are 'theological' in the sense that they are trying to interpret Christianity for their readers.

The explanation of the similarities between the Synoptic Gospels means that where they and John are different it is not three against one, but Mark against John. The following gives the main differences:

	Synoptic Gospels	John's Gospel
1. Beginning of the ministry:	After the arrest of John the Baptist	During John's ministry
2. Length of ministry:	One Passover Mk 14:1	Three Passovers Jhn 2:13, 6:4, 12:1
3. Place of ministry:	Galilee and the North except for the final week	Between Judea and Galilee
4. End of Ministry:	Last Supper was Passover Mk 14:1	Last Supper before the Passover Jhn 13:1, 18:28
5. Focus of ministry:	Kingdom of God	Eternal life
6. Controversies:	Interpretation of the law	Attitude towards Jesus
7. Messianic question:	Messianic secret not generally discussed	Public Messianic claim
8. Manner of teaching:	Parables and sayings	Allegories, speeches and replies to questions
9. Temple cleansing:	At end of ministry Mk 11:15–17	At beginning of ministry Jhn 2:13–16
10. Role of Jesus:	Proclaimer of the Kingdom	The Son sent by the Father

5.   The Characteristics of the Gospels

a Mark

According to an early Christian writer, Papias, (135 A.D.) Mark was the secretary of Peter in Rome. In 64 A.D. Peter died in the first persecution of Christians by Nero and Mark was requested to write down Peter's memories of Jesus so that they would not be lost. The Gospel is not a biography which traces Jesus' life as it happened but a collection of stories which Mark has linked together. Many of these were already in a definite oral form which has been used by Mark.

  i. The Gospel was written in poor Greek and it is suggested that the writer probably thought in Aramaic even though he wrote in Greek.

  ii. The style is concise but includes unimportant details which adds to the stories' authenticity eg. in the account of the feeding of the five thousand Mark includes a description of the people sitting in rows on the green grass (Mk 6:39–40).

  iii. Mark has used Aramaic words translated into Greek to point to the accuracy of his account, eg. 'Talitha Cumi' (Mk 5:41).

  iv. The link with Peter is shown by an apparent unflattering frankness about him which Matthew and Luke do not give.

  v. His underlying theme is that Jesus is the Messiah. This secret is gradually revealed through the Gospel.

  vi. There is no birth story, and no resurrection appearance in the oldest copies which end at 16:8.

The Gospel was probably written in Rome before 75 A.D. since it was used by Matthew and Luke. Scholars who think that Mark 13 was written before the fall of Jerusalem date the Gospel before 70 A.D. It was written to teach and encourage Gentile Christians. The absence of the birth stories can be explained by:

  a. Mark did not know them, which raises serious doubts about their authenticity.

or

  b. He placed no significance in them for his understanding of Jesus. The lack of resurrection stories in the oldest copies is a more serious problem. It is thought that Mark 16:9–20 was added by someone else before 170 A.D. It was not in the copies used by Matthew and Luke. Mark may not have regarded the Easter appearances as important because he expected Jesus to return as the Messiah to close history and judge all mankind.

The theme of the Gospel is the gradual realisation of the disciples that Jesus is the Messiah. The Gospel begins with their response to follow him. They witness his miracles and hear his teaching until eventually they believe that Jesus is not just a prophet like John the Baptist or a wonder-worker, but the Messiah promised by the Old Testament. At this point Jesus confirms their belief at Caesarea Philippi, but begins his final journey to Jerusalem. The disciples cannot face this final test. They desert Jesus to save themselves. The Gospel finishes with the instruction to go to Galilee to meet Jesus. It is a second chance which they must have taken since otherwise the Gospel could not have been written.

b Luke

The author is identified as the companion of Paul who also wrote Acts. The Gospel is the first part of a two part work which records the story of Christianity from its beginning in Bethlehem to its proclamation in Rome, which was regarded as the centre of the world. It was written in Rome or in Greece, at Corinth, between 75 and 85 A.D. It is a teaching gospel for Gentiles which has two purposes:

1. To deepen the faith of Christian readers.
2. To explain the faith to sympathetic non-Christian readers.

The main themes of Luke's Gospel are:

Jesus is the Messiah;

In dying, Jesus became Saviour of the world. He was rejected by his own people but accepted by the Gentiles;

The miracle stories are emphasised as in Matthew's Gospel;

Sympathy for all despised groups, eg. Samaritans, women and the poor;

To show that though Jesus was condemned as King of the Jews and executed as a rebel he was not a political leader, nor were Christians a threat to Roman power;

To encourage Christians to be ready for the return of Jesus even though this was delayed;

To show the importance of the Holy Spirit;

To show God's readiness to forgive sinners and his condemnation of the self-righteous;

The task of the disciples is to convert the world and not to wait for the Kingdom.

c Matthew

This is the only Gospel which was certainly written for Jewish Christians. One theory about its purpose is that it was written to be used in worship. Thus it can be divided into separate passages for use throughout the Christian year as the Church today has a lectionary (a list of Biblical readings for each Sunday). The pattern of Christian worship had developed out of synagogue worship. Christians had replaced the Jews as God's people. The Gospel was used first in Antioch and Palestine, but later became the main Gospel of the Church elsewhere. It was a text book for Christian leaders and teachers. It gave Jesus' new teaching in such a way that it clearly reinterpreted the old Jewish law.

    i. The five great discourses have been compared with the Torah (Mt 5–7; 10; 13; 18; 24).

    ii. It combines almost all of Mark (90%) with Q and the Special Matthew material. It is probable that most of Q was also included to give the fullest possible account of the life and teaching of Jesus.

    iii. There is guidance about how to organise the Church, how to settle disputes, and how to avoid false teaching. This advice is relevant to a settled community, and not one which will soon disappear when Jesus returns.

    iv. Jesus speaks of coming not to abolish the law but to fulfil it (Mt 5:17). He gives his new, more radical interpretation.

    v. The Gospel has eleven quotations from the Old Testament which are fulfilled in Jesus: 1:23; 2:6; 2:15; 2:18; 2:23; 4:15–16; 8:17; 12:18–21; 13:35; 21:5; 27:9

The Gospel was written in either Antioch or Palestine. It is usually dated between 80–100 A.D. since:

    a. Matthew used Mark.
    b. Mt 22:7 implies that Jerusalem had been destroyed.
    c. There is no expectation that the world will end soon.
    d. The Christian Church for which it was written is an established community.

As the Gospel depends on Mark and Q it could not have been written by Matthew the disciple. The name of the Gospel comes from a tradition that Matthew, the disciple collected 'logia' (sayings of Jesus) and prophecies about the Messiah which Jesus had fulfilled. These 'logia' were included in the Gospel as part of the material special to Matthew's Gospel.

The theme of the Gospel is the fulfillment of the Old Testament by Jesus. The birth stories emphasise his descent from David. The teaching of Jesus demands a more radical obedience to the Law. The Christian Church is the New Israel which is open to Gentiles as well as Jews.

Work Section

Section A

1. Why were the Gospels not written immediately after Jesus died?
2. Why were they eventually written?
3. What does 'synoptic' mean?
4. Which are the Synoptic Gospels?
5. What are pericopes?
6. What is the purpose of Biblical Criticism?
7. Which Gospel is usually thought to have been written first?
8. Which Gospel writers copied from Mark?
9. What does Q stand for?
10. What is Q thought to have contained?
11. Which Gospels use Q?
12. Why is it impossible to work out exactly what Q contained?
13. What is M?
14. What is L?
15. List five important differences between John's Gospel and the Synoptic Gospels.
16. What is the tradition about the author of Mark's Gospel?
17. Briefly list the six main characteristics of Mark's Gospel.
18. When is Mark's Gospel thought to have been written?
19. Which two important events in the life of Jesus are not recorded by Mark?
20. Summarise the theme of Mark's Gospel.
21. Which other book in the New Testament is thought to have been written by Luke?
22. Where, when, and why was Luke's Gospel written?
23. What was probably the purpose of Matthew's Gospel?
24. Summarise the five characteristics of Matthew's Gospel.
25. Where, and when, is Matthew thought to have been written?
26. What is the relationship between Matthew's Gospel and Matthew the disciple?
27. Summarise the theme of Matthew's Gospel.

Section B

28. Explain **a** the similarities and **b** the differences between the first three Gospels. Why is it thought that Mark's Gospel was written first? 14,6

29. Explain, with examples, what you understand by the Q passages in Gospels. What material is special to **a** Matthew and **b** Luke? 8,6,6

30. What are the characteristics of Luke's Gospel? Give examples to illustrate your answer. 20

31. 'Matthew's Gospel was written for Jewish Christians.' What evidence is there to support this statement? 20

Section C

32. Look up the following passages and decide what the relationship is between the three Gospels:
- *i* Mt 8:23–27; Mk 4:35–41; Lk 8:22–25
- *ii* Mt 10:26–33; Mk 8:31–38; Lk 12:2–12
- *iii* Mt 14:3–12; Mk 6:17–29; Lk 3:1–20
- *iv* Mt 2; Lk 2.

33. If one person copies from someone else's work, how can a good teacher tell which one has copied?

The Birth of Jesus

1. The Differences and Similarities between the two accounts

Matthew 1:18–2:23	*Luke* 1:26–56; 2:1–40
	Mary and Joseph were betrothed.
They lived in Bethlehem.	They lived in Nazareth.
An angel appeared to Joseph in a dream to say that he should marry Mary.	The Angel Gabriel appeared to Mary.
	The angel said that the child would be conceived by the Holy Spirit and would be called Jesus.
	Mary visited Elizabeth. The Magnificat is a poem in praise of God said by Mary.
	Mary and Joseph travelled to Bethlehem for the census.
Jesus was born in a house.	Jesus was born in a stable and laid in a manger.
Wise men followed a star. After visiting Herod they found Jesus in Bethlehem and offered gifts.	Shepherds visited Jesus after being told of his birth by angels.
The wise men were warned in a dream to return home a different way to avoid Herod. Joseph was warned to escape to Egypt.	

Herod ordered the deaths of boys under two around Bethlehem.	Jesus was circumcised after eight days and then taken to the Temple for the offering to be made. Simeon and Anna recognised him as the Messiah. The Nunc Dimittis is a poem said by Simeon.
Joseph was told by an angel in a dream that it was safe to return to Israel but is warned to settle in Nazareth.	Joseph and Mary returned to Nazareth with Jesus.

The birth stories are only found in Matthew and Luke. They come from the writers' own sources, M and L (see the 'Synoptic Problem' in Chapter 2). The stories are not in Mark's Gospel, either because he did not know them, or he did not think that they were important. John's Gospel begins with the coming of the 'Word'.

There are only a few similarities between Matthew and Luke's accounts:

    a. Jesus was conceived by God in a special way.
    b. He was born in Bethlehem.
    c. His parents were Mary and Joseph.
    d. He received special visitors.
    e. He was brought up in Nazareth.

2.   The Virgin Birth

Both Matthew and Luke describe Mary as a virgin but Luke gives it more emphasis. Matthew bases it on the prophecy from Isaiah which means 'girl'. 'Virgin' may be an inaccurate translation. There is no other example of virgin birth in either Jewish or pagan beliefs. There are legends of women conceiving after intercourse with gods but this is very different from the story in the Gospels. For Christians of the first century and for many people today, there is no difficulty in accepting the idea that God who created the universe could also fertilise an egg in Mary without intercourse. However Paul does not mention the virgin birth in his letters. The virgin birth may be a way of stressing that Jesus really was the son of God. It solves the problem for Jews who believed that all people were born in sin because Adam and Eve had disobeyed God, but Christians believed that Jesus lived a sinless life. If Jesus had been conceived in the normal way he could not have lived a sinless life.

3. Matthew
1:18–2:23

Matthew's account of the birth of Jesus is influenced by five Old Testament prophecies. These demonstrate that the birth of Jesus fulfilled God's plan. God tells people what to do through dreams.

a Date

The story is set in the reign of Herod the Great. If this is correct then it may be possible to work out the date.

> a. Herod died in 4 B.C. Therefore Jesus' birth must have been before 4 B.C.
> b. Herod ordered the killing of boys under the age of two years. Therefore it was probably before 6 B.C.
> c. Herod died whilst they were in Egypt.
> Therefore according to Matthew the birth was probably between 9–6 B.C.

b Joseph's dream
1:18–25

Mary and Joseph were betrothed. Girls were usually betrothed at the age of twelve. A marriage contract was drawn up stating the amount of the dowry and how much the wife would keep if her husband died or they were divorced. The betrothed girl was called a wife and was a widow if the man died. The betrothal could only be ended by divorce. During this time the girl remained in her father's house. The marriage took place one year later. In the dream the angel told Joseph that the child had been conceived by the Holy Spirit.

c The visit of the wise men
2:1–12

These were Persian astrologers and therefore Gentiles. The birth of great men was supposed to be marked by stars, eg. Alexander the Great and Augustus. The gifts give clues to the future life of Jesus:

a. Gold showed his Kingship.
b. Frankincense showed that he would be like a priest.
c. Myrrh showed that his death would be important. Myrrh was put on to dead bodies to hide the smell of decay.

d The Massacre and the escape to Egypt
2:13–23

The massacre of the two year old boys in Bethlehem is not recorded by other writers. Although it is consistent with Herod's reputation for cruelty, it may have developed as a parallel to Moses, (Exodus 2:1–10). He was saved despite Pharaoh's orders to kill all Hebrew boys. The implication is that Jesus is a greater Moses who will free God's people from slavery to sin as Moses had rescued them from slavery in Egypt.

e The Prophecies

i. 1:23. 'A virgin shall conceive and bear a son,
        and his name shall be called Emmanuel.' (Isaiah 7:14)

The word 'virgin' meant young woman or girl and did not necessarily mean that she had not experienced intercourse.

ii. 2:6 'And you, O Bethlehem, in the land of Judah,
        are by no means least among the rulers of Judah;
        for from you shall come a ruler
        who will govern my people Israel.' (Micah 5:2)

Bethlehem had been the home of David who was regarded as the greatest of all Kings. He ruled from 1025–990 B.C. The Messiah was expected to be a second and greater David.

iii. 2:18. 'A voice was heard in Ramah,
        wailing and loud lamentation,
        Rachel, weeping for her children,
        she refused to be consoled,
        because they were no more.' (Jeremiah 31:15)

Rachel was the favourite wife of Jacob and so the mother of the Jews who lived in the South.

iv. 2:15. 'Out of Egypt have I called my son.' (Hosea 11:1)

This is a reminder that the Jews had been slaves in Egypt.

v. 2:23 'He shall be called a Nazarene.'

This is not an exact quotation. It may have been confused with 'Nazirite'. These were men who devoted their lives to God.

4. Luke

a Jesus and John the Baptist
1:1–56

Luke links the birth of Jesus with that of John the Baptist but he stresses that Jesus was greater. (See Chapter 4 for a comparison of the two births.)

b The visit of the Angel Gabriel
1:26–38

Mary is told: a. She will conceive a son.
b. He will be called Jesus.
c. He will be great, the Son of God.
d. He will sit on the throne of David for ever.
When Mary asks how this will be possible, because she is a virgin, the angel says that the child will be conceived by the Holy Spirit.

c The Magnificat
1:46–55

This is similar to the song which Hannah sang when she took Samuel to the Temple. (1 Samuel 2:1–10)

d The birth in Bethlehem
2:1–7

Luke describes the birth of Jesus against a Gentile background. There is no historical evidence for a census being held in Palestine during the reign of Herod the Great, nor were people expected to return to their ancestral village for a census. The Roman governor of Syria, Quirinius, did conduct a census after Herod's successor, Archelaus, was sacked in 6 A.D. Luke is stressing the link between Jesus and David, and combining the traditions that Jesus was born in Bethlehem and brought up in Nazareth.

43

The birth of Jesus in a stable identifies him with those who were unwanted. Stables were often caves hollowed out of the cliffs.

e The visit of the Shepherds
2:8–20

Shepherds were despised by some strict Jews because they could not share fully in worship. But it must also be remembered that David, Abraham, and other founders of the Jewish nation were also shepherds. The Angel Gabriel tells the shepherds that 'a Saviour who is Christ the Lord' has been born in Bethlehem.

Verse 19 suggests the possibility that Luke's account can be traced back to Mary herself but it is probably Luke's way of claiming authority for his story.

f) The visit to the Temple
Luke 2:21–38

Jesus was circumcised and named on the eighth day in accordance with Jewish tradition. Luke records that Jesus was taken to the Temple 'to present him to the Lord.' This is a parallel to the dedication of Samuel (1 Samuel 1:26–28). However the visit was required by law to make the offering for the purification of Mary. Leviticus 12:6–8 laid down which offerings were to be made. If the family was too poor to afford a lamb, two doves could be offered instead. This was the offering which Mary made.

Simeon had been promised that he would not die until he saw the Messiah. Inspired by the Holy Spirit, he took Jesus in his arms and recited the poem which is now known as the Nunc Dimittis. Simeon warns Mary that 'a sword will pierce through your own soul also.' This is the first hint in Luke's Gospel of future suffering.

Anna was a prophetess who was eighty four years old. She prayed and fasted continually in the Temple. She gave thanks to God for the birth of Jesus who would redeem Israel.

g) The visit to Jerusalem when Jesus was twelve
Luke 2:41–52

Jesus went with his parents to Jerusalem to celebrate the Passover. He discussed questions with the teachers in the Temple who were amazed by his understanding. His unique relationship with God is stressed by Jesus' answer to his parents that he must be in his Father's house.

Work Section

Section A

1. Which Gospels contain the birth stories?
2. List the similarities between the two accounts.
3. Describe the visit of the angel to Joseph.
4. What does 'betrothed' mean?
5. How many wise men visited Jesus?
6. Describe the visit of the wise men to Jerusalem.
7. Why was Jesus taken to Egypt?
8. Describe the visit of the Angel Gabriel to Mary.
9. Summarise the Magnificat.
10. Why was Jesus born in Bethlehem according to Luke's Gospel?
11. What message did the Angel Gabriel and the host of angels give to the shepherds?
12. Why did Mary and Joseph visit Jerusalem shortly after the birth of Jesus?
13. Write out what Simeon said when he saw Jesus.
14. Which other person in the Temple recognised Jesus as the Messiah?
15. Describe the visit to Jerusalem when Jesus was twelve years old.

Section B

16. Describe the birth of Jesus according to **a** Matthew's Gospel, and **b** Luke's Gospel. 10,10

17. How do the accounts of the birth of Jesus demonstrate that he was to be a special person? 20

18. What part was played by **a** angels, **b** dreams, in the account of the birth of Jesus? 10,10

19. Which Old Testament prophecies does Matthew use in his account of the birth of Jesus? How do they influence Matthew's story? 10,10

20. Describe the parts played in the accounts of the birth of Jesus by, **a** Caesar Augustus, **b** Joseph, **c** Elisabeth, **d** Simeon and **e** Mary. 2,6,2,4,6

21. Describe the visit of the wise men to Jerusalem and Bethlehem. What significance has been attached to the gifts which they presented? 14,6

22. Describe the events which took place in and around Bethlehem from the arrival of Mary and Joseph to the return of the shepherds to their flocks. How do these events demonstrate that Jesus' concern would be for sinners and those who were despised? 14,6

23. Give an account of **a** the Magnificat, **b** The Benedictus and **c** the Nunc Dimittis. 7,7,6

24. What did the Angel Gabriel say to **a** Zechariah about his son, and **b** to Mary about the birth of Jesus? What does John's Gospel say about The Word? 7,7,6

25. Why was belief in the Virgin Birth important for early Christians? What problems does it present for Christians today? 12,8

Section C

26. The traditional story of Christmas mixes together the two Biblical stories and legends. Ask five people to describe the birth of Jesus. Note any details which are not found in the Gospels.

27. Why do you think the New Testament includes two versions of the birth of Jesus which are so different?

28. Why is it impossible to give an historical account of the birth of Jesus?

29. Read Hannah's song in 1 Samuel 2:1–10 and list the points which are similar to the Magnificat.

30. Read 'The Place of Women' in Chapter One and work out how old Mary probably was.

John the Baptist

1. His birth
Luke 1:5–25

Zechariah was a priest of the division of Abijah. Priests were divided into twenty four groups and each group took a turn to perform a week's duties in the Temple. One priest was chosen by drawing lots to make the incense offering. Zechariah was making the offering when the Angel Gabriel appeared. This story is similar to that of Abraham and Sarah who were also old and childless.

Zechariah is given information about his son:
a. He will be called John.
b. Many will rejoice at his birth.
c. He will be great before God.
d. He will not drink wine. (This may mean that John was a Nazirite, see Numbers 6:1–21. Nazirite rules were a protest against heathen religions.)
e. He will be filled with the Holy Spirit.
f. He will turn Israel back to God.
g. He will be filled with the spirit of Elijah. (Some Jews believed that Elijah would return to prepare the way for the Messiah.)
h. He will prepare the way of the Lord.

Zechariah did not believe the angel and so was struck dumb as a punishment. (This also happens to Daniel in Daniel 10:15.)

2. The naming and the benedictus
Luke 1:57–80

It was usual for a son to be named after his father, but Elizabeth wanted to call him John. Zechariah confirmed the name by writing it down. The Benedictus, sung by Zechariah, is a parallel to the Magnificat. It is made up of Old Testament prophecies.
a. John will fulfil the promise given to Abraham that Israel will be saved from her enemies.

b. He will be the prophet promised by Malachi (4:5), who will prepare the way of the Lord.

c. He will give knowledge of salvation and forgiveness of sins.

d. He will be a light to those in darkness (Isaiah 9:2).

Similarities and Differences between the birth of John and Jesus.

Similarities:

a. Both births are announced by the Angel Gabriel.

b. Songs are sung: The Magnificat by Mary, the Benedictus by Zechariah.

c. Information is given by the angel about their names and future lives.

d. Both births are miraculous: Mary is a virgin, Elizabeth is barren.

e. They are both circumcised on the eighth day, (according to Luke).

Differences:

a. The angel did not appear to Elizabeth.

b. Elizabeth was old and barren, but Mary was a virgin.

c. John was conceived naturally whereas Jesus was conceived by the Holy Spirit.

d. There are no Old Testament parallels for the birth of Jesus but the birth of Samuel and Isaac are similar to that of John.

e. Zechariah does not believe and is struck dumb whereas Joseph (in Matthew) and Mary (in Luke) believe immediately.

f. There is no account of unusual visitors at the birth of John.

3. John's Preaching
Mark 1:1–8; Matthew 3:1–12; Luke 3:1–18; John 1:6–8, 19–36

There has been some speculation that John was an Essene. The Essenes were a Jewish sect who lived in remote communities. It has been suggested that Qumran was one. They believed that they were the true people of God (the remnant). They were ascetics (leading lives of self-denial). They were not allowed to marry or to have possessions. They obeyed the Jewish law strictly*. John also lived an ascetic life, eating locusts (some commentators think that he ate locust beans, but the Jewish law did allow them to eat some locusts, Leviticus 11:22), and wild honey and wearing a coat of camel's hair and a leather belt. (This differs from the Essenes who wore white robes.) John baptised people at one of the fords of

*Admission to the community was by ritual baptism which was repeated each year on the Day of Atonement

the River Jordan, probably only eight miles from Qumran. However John's message differed from that of the Essenes because he preached forgiveness for everyone who repented†. The Essenes would have had nothing to do with the tax collectors and sinners whom John attracted to him. John urged the people to repent because the Judgement was imminent. He was preparing the way for one who was greater than he was, who would gather in the final harvest and baptise with fire and the Holy Spirit. Mark adds that John said he was not fit to unfasten Jesus' sandals (Mk 1:7).

John gave advice to various groups:

a. Pharisees and Sadducees should not think that they have no need to repent because they are descendents of Abraham. God could make children of Abraham out of the stones on the ground (Mt 3:7–10).

b. Tax collectors should collect no more than was due (Lk 3:12–13).

c. Soldiers should not rob people or make false accusations (Lk 3:14).

d. Those who have two coats and food must share with those who have nothing (Lk 3:11).

N.B. There are two other suggestions about John's Baptism.

a. Jews baptised proselytes (Gentile converts to Judaism). John's baptism may be an extension of this.

b. There was a Jewish tradition that at Sinai the Jews prepared for receiving God's Law by immersing themselves in water. (This is mentioned in 1 Corinthians 10:1–2) The Jews in the wilderness were regarded as a model for the people who would be recognised by God at the end of time. Therefore, by accepting John's baptism the people were preparing themselves for the end of time.

4. The Baptism of Jesus
Mark 1:9–11; Matthew 3:13–17; Luke 3:21–22; John 1:29–34

The four Gospels and Acts record that Jesus was baptised. It is highly unlikely that the story would have been made up since it raises certain difficulties.

†His baptism was once and for all, not repeated every year

a. Jesus is subordinating himself to John.
b. Since Jesus was regarded as sinless he would not need to be baptised for the forgiveness of sins.

Matthew records that John was reluctant to baptise Jesus but Jesus says that it must be so in order to fulfil all righteousness. Jesus is thus associating himself with the people who needed to repent in order to obtain righteousness.

The traditional idea of Jesus being immersed in the water by John is unlikely. The Greek word which is used means 'to immerse oneself'. It is likely that Luke is correct when he describes Jesus as immersing himself along with other people when John gave the sign (Lk 3:21). John was acting as a witness as in the baptism of proselytes. The heavens open and Jesus is described as receiving the spirit. This is compared with a dove, possibly meaning that it descended with a gentle sound like a dove. The heavenly voice says a mixture of Psalm 2:7, 'You are my son, today I have begotten you' and Isaiah 42:1 'Behold my servant, whom I uphold, my chosen, in whom my soul delights.' The quotation from the Psalms was used when a King was crowned and the one from Isaiah described God's choice of the suffering servant. Some scholars think that the quotation was only taken from Isaiah since the Greek word for 'servant' also means 'son'. This would put all the stress on Jesus' recognition that he was to be the suffering servant and not a kingly Messiah.

5. John's Question to Jesus
Luke 7:18–23; Matthew 11:2–6

John was probably imprisoned in the fortress of Machaerus by the Dead Sea. He had criticised Herod's marriage to Herodias, who was the wife of his half brother. This was not allowed under Jewish law (Leviticus 18:16). There is no evidence that Herodias' husband had divorced her but Roman law allowed a wife to divorce her husband. Jesus was not the sort of Messiah that John expected. The question wants Jesus to confirm whether he is the Messiah. Jesus does not give a direct answer but points to the evidence of healings. These show that God is working through Jesus.

6. Jesus' Description of John
Matthew 11:7–19; Luke 7:24–35

Jesus says of John:
- a. He is more than a prophet.
- b. He has fulfilled the words of Malachi (3:1) by preparing the way.
- c. He is the greatest of all men.
- d. The least in the Kingdom of God is greater than John. John is no longer the prophet of the future because he belongs to the time when the prophecies are being fulfilled. John belongs to the old age of the law which has now given way to the new age of Jesus.
- e. He has brought in the time of salvation.
- f. He is Elijah.

Jesus compared the people with the children playing and arguing in the market place. They thought that John the Baptist was too gloomy because he was an ascetic, but Jesus was too worldly because he ate with sinners.

7. John's Death
Mark 6:17–29; Matthew 14:1–12

According to Josephus, Herod Antipas executed John for political reasons. When Herod married Herodias he divorced his Arabian wife. This caused a war against the Arabians which Herod lost. The Jews interpreted their defeat as a punishment from God, therefore Herod executed John. An execution without trial was against the Jewish Law, as was beheading which was a Roman and Greek method of execution.

It is impossible to make this account agree with the story in the Gospels. It is usually assumed on the basis of Luke 3:1 that John the Baptist was executed in 29–30 A.D., but Herod was not defeated by the Arabians until 37 A.D. Another difficulty is that Salome, the daughter of Herodias, was married to Philip, Herod's half brother. Considering the low status of dancing women, it is surprising that a princess who was married (or even a widow since Philip died in 32 A.D.), would have danced at court. The story recalls the Old Testament story of how Esther pleased the King (Ahasuerus) and he offered her anything up to half his kingdom. Herod Antipas could not have kept his promise to give her 'half his kingdom' (Mk 6:23) because he ruled by permission of the Romans.

8.   The Relationship between Jesus and John

Jesus and John both preached in the open, unlike other Jewish teachers. They rejected the self righteous and welcomed sinners who repented. Jesus announced the coming of the Kingdom whereas John stressed the coming Judgement.

The Synoptic Gospels only mention one meeting between Jesus and John, at Jesus' baptism. John's Gospel (3:22–4:3) says that Jesus baptised alongside John at the beginning of his ministry. (John 4:2 is thought to have been added later because the early Church would have found it difficult to accept that Jesus had worked with John.) If Jesus had baptised people it is easier to understand why the early Church began to baptise. It is very unlikely that Jesus and John would have only met once, but the early Church would have wanted to avoid any suggestion that Jesus had been a follower of John. According to John 1:35–39, Jesus' first disciples had been disciples of John the Baptist.

Work Section

Section A

1. How does Luke describe the characters of Zechariah and Elizabeth?
2. Where was Zechariah and what was he doing when the angel of the Lord appeared?
3. Why did Zechariah doubt what the angel said and how was he punished?
4. Describe what happened when John was named.
5. How did John differ from the Essenes?
6. What did John eat and what did he wear?
7. Where did John baptise people?
8. What did John teach?
9. In John's Gospel what was John the Baptist's reply to the question of the priests and levites sent by the Jews from Jerusalem?
10. Describe the baptism of Jesus and explain what difficuties are raised by this incident.
11. When John was in prison what was the question which he sent his disciples to ask Jesus, and what was Jesus' reply?
12. Why did John criticise Herod Antipas and Herodias?
13. What did Herod promise Herodias' daughter and why?
14. What did Herodias' daughter ask for?
15. What historical difficulties are raised by this incident?
16. Assess the similarities and differences between the teaching of John and that of Jesus.

Section B

17. Relate **a** the Magnificat and **b** the Benedictus. How did John prepare the way for Jesus? 6,6,7

18. Describe the visit of the angel to **a** Zechariah and **b** Mary. How were the prophecies of the angel fulfilled? 7,7,6

19. In what ways were the events of the birth of John the Baptist and the birth of Jesus **a** similar and **b** different? 10,10

20. What advice did John give to those who came to be baptised? Describe the baptism of Jesus. 12,8

21. What was the question which John sent his disciples to ask Jesus? How did Jesus reply? What did Jesus say about John the Baptist? 4,4,12

22. What is recorded in the Synoptic Gospels about the life and work of John the Baptist? What extra information is found in John's Gospel? 15,5

Section C

23. What problems are raised by the relationship between Jesus and John?

24. What does Acts 18:24–19:7 say about the disciples of John the Baptist?

25. Why do you think Jesus chose to be baptised?

26. On which other occasion is God described as speaking to Jesus from a cloud? (Mk 9:7)

27. For further information about the Essenes read *The Dead Sea Scrolls in English* G. Vermes.

Jesus, the Messiah

The Gospels use several titles to explain the mission and nature of Jesus. The meaning of these titles will help us to understand what the Gospel writers thought of Jesus and also offer clues to what Jesus thought of himself. Titles such as 'Messiah' are now identified exclusively with Jesus. However they were first used by Jews. An examination of their Jewish meaning will help us to explain their importance in the New Testament.

1. 'Messiah'

The word 'Messiah' means 'anointed'. In Israel, high priests and Kings were anointed with oil as a sign that God had chosen them. 'Christ' is the Greek word for 'Messiah'. The idea of the Messiah developed after the Jews had returned from exile in Babylon in the sixth century B.C. They hoped for a leader who would restore the glory of the reign of David. The Messiah would be a descendant of David, chosen by God, to rule as King. Prophets such as Zechariah and Micah described his reign as being one of peace. However the popular hope at the time of Jesus, especially amongst the Zealots, was that the Messiah would be an earthly warrior who would free the people from their enemies and especially the Romans and their supporters.

According to the Synoptic Gospels, Jesus did not speak of himself as the Messiah. He rejected the idea of being a military Messiah but he did fulfil some of the prophecies of a peaceful Messiah, eg. he rode into Jerusalem on a new colt to fulfil Zechariah 9:9. At Caesarea Philippi Jesus accepted Peter's confession that he was the Messiah but he warned the disciples not to tell anyone, (Mk 8:27–30). Jesus avoided using the word 'Messiah' because he did not accept the popular meaning of the title. There are hints in the Gospels that some people hoped that Jesus would be a military leader, (eg. Jhn 6:15). The temptation to worship the devil can be interpreted as Jesus' rejection of military power. When Jesus used a title he preferred 'Son of Man'.

2. 'Son of Man'

This is the only title in the Gospels which Jesus uses of himself and which is thought by most scholars to be historically true. In some cases it may have originally only meant 'man' and the Gospel writers changed it into the title 'Son of Man'. The Jewish phrase, 'Bar Nasa' (Bar = son of; nasa = man) was a way of referring to 'man'. The phrase has been translated literally as 'Son of Man'. The title is not explained in the Gospels.

'Son of Man' is used for the first time in Daniel's vision (Daniel 7:13). Daniel sees four great beasts appear from the sea. A fifth, like 'the Son of Man' appears in heaven, with the clouds. He is given power and glory. In Rabbinic literature the Son of Man was identified with the Messiah.

Jesus uses the title 'Son of Man' in the third person. It is usually applied to the future. He therefore distinguishes between himself and the Son of Man. Jesus may mean that after the resurrection he will become the Son of Man, and the vision of Daniel will be realised. The Son of Man will appear suddenly in the clouds, with his angels, to judge the world.

3. The Suffering Servant

Jesus does not use the title 'Suffering Servant' but he does refer to the prophecies of Isaiah and combines them with the idea of the Son of Man. A description of the suffering servant is given in Isaiah 53:3, 'He was despised and rejected by men; a man of sorrows and acquainted with grief; and as one from whom men hide their faces he was despised, and we esteemed him not.' His suffering is not because of his own sin but is a punishment for the sins of others. According to the first Christians Jesus lived a completely sinless life but suffered and died, like the suffering servant, on behalf of other people. This is called the Atonement. 'The Son of Man came . . . to give his life as a ransom for many.' (Mk 10:45) In the story of Jesus' baptism the Messiah is linked with the suffering servant when the voice from heaven says, 'Thou are my beloved son; with thee I am well pleased.' This is a combination of Psalm 2:7 which is a coronation psalm and Isaiah 42:1 which refers to the suffering servant. This link was not made in Jewish literature.

4.   The Temptations
Mark 1:12–13; Matthew 4:1–11; Luke 4:1–13

The temptations are a way of introducing the story of Jesus' mission. After his baptism he must decide how he will use the power given to him by God to teach people about the Kingdom. The word 'tempt' is better translated as 'test'. If Jesus is to succeed he must have an absolute obedience to God's will despite the suffering this may involve. Mark gives a brief summary which mentions Jesus living amongst the wild beasts. This may refer to the Jewish hope that one day men and animals would live peacefully together as in the Garden of Eden (Genesis 2:19, Isaiah 11:6–9). It was believed that all people were sinful because they were descended from Adam and Eve who had disobeyed God. Jesus' obedience to God will cancel out Adam's sin. The wilderness was thought to be where evil spirits lived. It was also thought to be where the Messiah would come from. 'Forty' is a symbolic number for periods of oppression (eg. the flood lasted forty days, the Jews were in the wilderness for forty years). The image of the devil can be explained as a symbol of the evil which exists in the world. The temptations can be understood as being in Jesus' mind rather than an actual conversation with the devil.

i)   'If you are the Son of God, command these stones to become loaves of bread.' Jesus replied, 'It is written, "man shall not live by bread alone but by every word that proceeds from the mouth of God."' (Deuteronomy 8:3)

This is to test whether Jesus will use his power selfishly. The ability to turn stones into bread can be seen as a symbol for creating anything that he wants. Many people would follow him if he gave them bread but they would have followed him for the bread and not for the truth of his teaching. If could be argued that the feeding miracles suggest that Jesus later accepted this temptation. However the people had not followed him to be fed but to hear his teaching.

N.B. The order of the last two temptations is different in Matthew and Luke. We shall follow Matthew's order.

ii)   The devil took Jesus to the pinnacle of the Temple and said, 'If you are the Son of God, throw yourself down; for it is written, "He will give his angels charge over you" and "on their hands they will bear you up, lest you strike your foot against a stone."' (The devil quotes from Psalm 91:11–12). Jesus replies, 'Again it is written, "You shall not tempt the Lord your God."' (Deuteronomy 6:16)

This is to test whether Jesus will use his power to do spectacular feats in order to attract attention. He would have created great interest and gathered large crowds but they would not necessarily have listened and believed. Jesus did not give in to this temptation when he performed miracles. Miracles were the result of faith in Jesus. He often told people to keep the miracle secret. On some occasions he left towns in order to escape crowds who came only to be healed.

iii)   The devil took Jesus to a very high mountain and showed him all the kingdoms of the world. He said. 'All these I will give you, if you fall down and worship me.' Jesus replies, 'Begone Satan! for it is written, "You shall worship the Lord your God and him only shall you serve."' (Deuteronomy 6:13)

This is to test whether Jesus will use evil powers to achieve his mission. Jesus could have been the kind of military leader that many people wanted. Jesus rejected this temptation because the Kingdom of God comes through faith, love and obedience to God. Luke describes all the kingdoms of the world as belonging to the devil. Jesus must overcome the devil in order to free people from the power of evil.

The Gospels give three other occasions when Jesus is tempted to avoid suffering.

a. At Caesarea Philippi Jesus told his disciples that the Son of Man must suffer and be killed, and after three days rise again. When Peter objected to this, Jesus said, 'Get behind me, Satan! For you are not on the side of God, but of men.' (Mk 8:27–33)

b. In the Garden of Gethsemane Jesus prays that he may not have to suffer but he accepts God's will. (Mk 14:36)

c. When Jesus is on the cross the chief priests and scribes say, 'He saved others; he cannot save himself. Let the Christ, the King of Israel, come down now from the cross, that we may see and believe.' (Mk 15:31–32)

5.   Peter's Confession at Caesarea Philippi
Matthew 16:13–20; Mark 8:27–9:1; Luke 9:18–22

This incident took place at Caesarea Philippi in Mark and Matthew, but the place is not mentioned in Luke. It marks the end of Jesus' teaching in Galilee and the beginning of the journey to Jerusalem. Jesus asked the disciples two questions:

a. 'Who do men say that I am?' (Matthew has 'The Son of Man' instead of 'I')
   The disciples reply that the people said that he was John the Baptist, Elijah, or one of the other prophets. (Matthew adds 'Jeremiah')

b. 'Who do you say that I am?'
   Peter replied that he was the Messiah.

Jesus accepts this title but refers to himself as the Son of Man, because he does not want to identify himself with the expectation of a military Messiah. In Matthew, Peter was praised for his insight and told that he would be the rock on which the Church would be built. (The Greek word 'petros' means 'rock'.) Jesus told them not to tell anyone and went on to describe how the Son of Man would be rejected by the Jewish leaders, and be killed, but he would rise on the third day. Peter told Jesus that this could not happen. Jesus saw this as another temptation not to suffer and he addressed Peter as 'Satan', telling him that he thought as men thought not as God. Peter could not understand Jesus' mission as a suffering Messiah.

6. The Transfiguration
Matthew 17:1–13; Mark 9:2–13; Luke 9:28–36

This took place six days after Peter's confession, (Luke has eight days). Six days was traditionally the length of time needed to purify oneself before approaching God. The Gospels do not mention the name of the mountain. It could possibly have been Mount Tabor or Mount Hermon. The word 'transfigured' means 'to be transformed', 'to change one's form'. Jesus' human appearance was temporarily changed to the glorious form that he would possess after he was exalted to heaven. Mark stresses the supernatural element by adding that Jesus' clothes became whiter than any earthly bleach could produce. The Jews believed that characters from the Old Testament would appear to take part in the events leading up to the end of the world. Moses represents the law, and Elijah the Prophets. Their appearance also witnessed to the fact that Jesus was not a false prophet. The voice speaking from the cloud confirmed that he was the Son of God. This was the Shekinah cloud which indicated the presence of God. The early Christians also believed that Jesus would return in the clouds in the Glory of God.

There are two possible reasons why Peter asked if he should build three shelters (tabernacles):

a. He wanted to prolong the experience.
b. The Jews believed that one day God would be with them as he had been in the wilderness, when they lived in tabernacles. Peter was offering to build the shelters which God was expected to share with men in the age to come.

Jesus warned the disciples not to tell anyone what had happened until the Son of Man had risen from the dead. He said that Elijah had already come, meaning John the Baptist.

The Transfiguration has been interpreted in various ways:

a. It may be a symbolic story to affirm that Jesus is the Messiah.
b. It may have been a vision experienced by Peter, James and John.
c. It may have been a resurrection appearance which has been put earlier in the Gospel story as a hint of what was to come.

7. Jesus' Rejection at Nazareth
Matthew 13:53–58; Mark 6:1–6; Luke 4:16–30

The people of Nazareth could not recognise the importance of Jesus because they knew him as 'the carpenter, the son of Mary, and brother of James, and Joses, and Judas and Simon.' The Jews always introduced a man by reference to his father, not his mother. This would have been the case even if the man's father was dead. It is possible that Mark is stressing that God is the father of Jesus. The brothers and sisters of Jesus are mentioned. Since some people maintain that Mary was always a virgin, they have said that these were half brothers and sisters or cousins. Jesus explains their rejection by quoting the proverb, 'A prophet is not without honour, except in his own country, and among his own kin, and in his own house.' Mark records that Jesus was unable to do mighty works in Nazareth, except for healing a few sick people, because of their lack of faith.

Luke adds a description of Jesus' teaching in the synagogue. He reads from Isaiah 61:1–2 and says that the prophecies have now been fulfilled. He illustrates the proverb about a prophet not being honoured by his own people, by referring to the stories of Elijah and Elisha. Luke ends his account with an attempt to throw Jesus off a hill but he passed through them and went away.

Jesus' statement that the prophecies of Isaiah were being fulfilled was a claim to be the Messiah. The crowd may have wanted to throw Jesus off the hill in order to stone him for blasphemy.

Other occasions when Jesus is seen to be the Messiah are:

Jesus' baptism. (Mt 3:13–17; Mk 1:9–11; Lk 3:21–22; Jhn 1:28–34)

The healing of the blind man, (who calls out that Jesus is the Son of David) (Mt 9:27–31; Mk 10:46–52; Lk 18:35–43)

Jesus' entry into Jerusalem. (Mt 21:8–11; Mk 11:7–10; Lk 19:35–38; Jhn 12:12–15)

The trial in front of the Sanhedrin (when Jesus openly admits that he is the Messiah). (Mt 26:57–68; Mk 14:53–65; Lk 22:66–71; Jhn 18:12–24)

The Samaritan woman at the well. (Jhn 4:7–42)

The question in the Temple. (Jhn 10:22–39)

Work Section

Section A

1. Why are titles such as 'Messiah' and 'Son of Man' not explained by the Gospel writers?
2. What do the words 'Messiah' and 'Christ' mean?
3. What was the Jewish expectation of the Messiah?
4. In the Synoptic Gospels why did Jesus not openly speak of himself as the Messiah?
5. According to the Gospels, which title did Jesus use to refer to himself?
6. What was the origin of the phrase 'Son of Man'?
7. How does Jesus use the title 'Son of Man'?
8. Briefly describe the suffering servant.
9. How did Jesus fulfil the prophecies of the suffering servant?
10. Where was Jesus when he was tempted by the devil?
11. What is the significance of the wilderness?
12. Why was Jesus hungry?
13. What was the first temptation and how did Jesus reply?
14. Where was Jesus when the devil tempted him to throw himself down?
15. Where did the devil take Jesus in order to tempt him to worship him?
16. What does Matthew's Gospel say happened after the devil left Jesus?
17. What does Luke, say about the devil's departure?
18. Why might Peter's confession be considered as a turning point in Mark's Gospel?
19. According to Matthew's Gospel, what did Jesus tell Peter after his confession that Jesus was the Messiah?
20. Why did Jesus later say to Peter, 'Get behind me Satan'?
21. Which disciples witnessed the Transfiguration?
22. What does Peter ask Jesus if he should do whilst they are on the mountain?

23. How does Matthew describe Jesus' appearance when he was transfigured?

24. What does the voice from the cloud say?

25. On what other occasion is a voice heard from a cloud?

26. Describe the conversation between Jesus and his disciples as they came down from the mountain.

27. Why did the people at Nazareth reject Jesus?

28. Which two examples from the Old Testament did Jesus use to show how prophets were rejected by their own people?

Section B

29. What sort of Messiah did some of the Jews expect. How did Jesus demonstrate that he was different from their expectation? 8,12

30. On what occasions in the Synoptic Gospels is Jesus represented as accepting that he was the Messiah? 20

31. Explain the importance of the title 'Son of Man'. How does Jesus combine this title with the prophecies about the suffering servant? 10,10

32. Describe the temptations which Jesus overcame in the wilderness. How would Jesus' ministry have been different if he had not rejected them? 12,8

33. What temptations did Jesus face during his life, and how did he overcome them? 20

34. 'Who do men say that the Son of Man is?' Give a detailed account of the discussion which took place after this question. Briefly describe two other occasions when Jesus was acknowledged as the Messiah. 12,4,4

35. What incident concerning the Messiahship of Jesus took place at Caesarea Philippi? Why was Jesus reluctant to declare openly that he was the Messiah? What title did he use instead? 8,6,6

36. Describe the events on the mountain when Jesus was transfigured. Describe another occasion when the voice from a cloud spoke to Jesus. 10,10

37. Describe the occasion when Jesus entered the synagogue at Nazareth. Why were the people so angry with him, and how did they express their anger? 8,8,4

Section C

38. Look up the title 'Son of Man' and 'Messiah' in a concordance and list the most important occasions when they are used in the Gospels.

39. The temptations can be understood as Jesus' rejection of using bribery, stunts, or evil methods eg. force. How should a teacher in school today respond to these same temptations?

40. Do you think that the miracles of the feeding of the five thousand, and four thousand, are an acceptance of the temptation to turn stones into bread?

41. How would Jesus have been accepting the temptation to worship the devil if he had been the popular Messiah expected by some of the Jews?

42. Read the description of the suffering servant in Isaiah 42:1–9 and explain how Jesus fulfilled the prophecies.

43. Read Isaiah 53.

44. Read Daniel's vision in Daniel, chapter seven.

Discipleship

1. The Twelve Disciples

'Disciple' means 'one who learns'. The number twelve represents the twelve tribes of Israel. There are four lists giving the names of the disciples, Mt 10:2–4, Mk 3:16–19, Lk 6:14–16, Acts 1:13. Mark and Matthew include Thaddaeus but Luke and Acts have Judas son of James instead of Thaddaeus. It is possible that after Judas Iscariot betrayed Jesus, Judas son of James was called by the nick-name Thaddaeus, since the name Judas would have been hated by the early Church. The disciples are called to: a. be with Jesus,

      b. preach,

      c. cast out demons. (Mk 3:14–15)

1.	Simon Peter	In Matthew, Simon is not called Peter until after his confession at Caesarea Philippi.
2.	James }	the sons of Zebedee,
3.	John }	nicknamed Boanerges (the sons of thunder)
4.	Andrew	the brother of Simon Peter
5.	Philip	
6.	Bartholomew	
7.	Matthew	The tax collector who is called Levi in Mark and Luke is identified with Matthew, the disciple, in Matthew's Gospel.
8.	Thomas	
9.	James son of Alphaeus	
10.	Thaddaeus (Judas son of James)	
11.	Simon the Canaanite (a Zealot)	
12.	Judas Iscariot	This may mean 'man of Kerioth', ie. from Judaea, or it may mean 'dagger-man'.

2.   The Call of the first disciples
Matthew 4:18–22; Mark 1:16–20; Luke 5:1–11; John 1:40–42

Simon and his brother Andrew were fishing. James and John were mending their nets. The phrase 'fishers of men' comes from Jeremiah 16:16. It shows that the disciples are to bring people back to God. Luke includes the miracle of the full net of fish to show that they will be successful. John's account is set in Judaea. Andrew was a disciple of John the Baptist.

3.   The Mission of the Twelve
Matthew 10:5–15; Mark 6:7–13; Luke 9:1–6

The disciples are sent out in pairs because,
a. they could protect each other on lonely roads.
b. because the evidence of two witnesses could be trusted, (Deut 17:6)
They were not to take:
a. Bread as they should trust God to provide for them.
b. A bag as this could be to collect money in, or to carry food.
c. Money in their belts. It was usual to carry small change in a belt.
d. Two tunics. This could mean that they were not to take a robe and a cloak, (a cloak was necessary to spend nights in the open air), or it could mean that they were not to carry a spare inner garment.
N.B. Matthew and Luke also forbid a staff and sandals. Mark may have allowed these because they would have been used by missionaries from his Church.
The disciples are told to stay in the same house until they leave each village. If they are not received hospitably as they leave they must shake the dust from their feet to warn the people that they had rejected God's Kingdom. Strict Jews did this when they returned to Israel after being abroad.

4.   The Mission of the Seventy
Luke 10:1–24

N.B. some manuscripts say seventy-two.
This symbolises the mission to the world because it was believed that there were only seventy nations. It is very similar to the mission of the

twelve. The seventy are forbidden to greet anyone on the road. This is a strange command because Jews believed that God's peace was passed on by such greetings. It could mean that they were not to waste time by joining other travellers. It was common to travel with other people as protection against robbers but they would have travelled more slowly. The seventy return in triumph.

5. Renunciation
Mark 10:28–31; Luke 14:25–35

In Mark, Peter says that they have left everything to follow Jesus. In Luke, Jesus tells the rich young ruler to sell all his possessions, give the money to the poor, and follow him. The Essenes also renounced their possessions but they gave them to the community whereas Jesus said that they were to be given to the poor. In Mark, Jesus says that they will receive what they have lost a hundred times over. They will be part of the family of which God is the Father.

In Luke, Jesus illustrates his teaching with two short parables:

a. A man who is building a tower has to first calculate the cost.
b. A king who is going to war will work out whether his army is strong enough, otherwise he will make peace.

In the same way it is necessary to calculate the cost of being a disciple of Jesus.

6. The Suffering of the Disciples
Matthew 10:38–39; Luke 14:27

Jesus seems to have expected that his disciples would suffer after his death. His disciples are warned that they must be willing to take up their cross and follow him. This teaching must date from after the crucifixion. Before the death of Jesus the cross was only associated with the execution of thieves and slaves.

7. Humility and Service
Matthew 18:1–6; Mark 9:33–37; Luke 9:46–48; John 13:12–20

a. Jesus tells the disciples that if anyone would be first he must be last. The only way to become great was by serving others. (In

John's Gospel, Jesus illustrates his teaching by washing the feet of his disciples.) There was a similar Rabbinic phrase, 'God will exalt him who humbles himself, God will humble him who exalts himself.' Jesus uses a child as an example for the disciples to follow. This may be because children, are humble, or pure, or Jesus may be saying that the disciples must learn, like a child, to use the word 'abba' (daddy) for God. Jesus says that anyone who causes a child to stumble should have a mill-stone hung round his neck and be thrown into the sea. This was a common Roman punishment.

b. (Mt 20:20–28, Mk 10:35–45) In Mark, James and John ask Jesus if they can sit on either side of him when Jesus comes into his glory. (In Matthew it is their mother who makes the request.) Jesus gives two answers: It is not in Jesus' power to decide; the places of honour in the Kingdom depend on a martyr's death. Seats on either side of the host were the most honourable. The disciples may have been thinking of seats next to Jesus at the Messianic banquet. Jesus asks if they can accept his cup and his baptism which are symbols of suffering. Acts 12:2 records the martyrdom of James under Herod Agrippa. According to some accounts, John is thought to have lived at Ephesus when Trajan was Emperor, 70–85 A.D.

8. The commissioning
Matthew 28:16–20; Luke 24:44–53; Acts 1:1–14

The disciples are told to preach repentance and forgiveness of sins. In Matthew, Jesus meets them in Galilee and they are told to make disciples of all the nations, baptising them in the name of the Father, the Son, and the Holy Spirit. In Luke and Acts, Jesus meets the disciples in Jerusalem. He promises to give them the Holy Spirit.

Work Section

Section A

1. How does the list of the twelve disciples differ in Matthew and Mark? How can this difference be explained?
2. Why did Jesus call disciples?
3. Which disciples were brothers?
4. Describe the call of the tax collector in Mt 9:9. What is he called in Mark and Luke?
5. Why was Simon the Canaanite an unusual disciple for Jesus to choose?
6. According to the Synoptic Gospels, who were the first four disciples to be called and what was their occupation?
7. How is John's account of the call of the first disciples different · from that found in the Synoptic Gospels?
8. What is the significance of the phrase 'fishers of men'?
9. Relate the miracle included by Luke in the story of the call of the first disciples.
10. Describe the mision of the twelve.
11. What instructions did Jesus give to the seventy before they were sent out?
12. What is Jesus' reply when Peter says that they have left everything in order to follow Jesus?
13. Why does Jesus use a child as an example for the disciples to follow?
14. In Matthew's Gospel what does Jesus instruct his disciples to do when he meets them in Galilee for the last time?

Section B

15. What do the Synoptic Gospels record about the call of the first disciples? What further information is found in John's Gospel?
    12,8

16. Give an account of the mission of the twelve and the seventy. 10,10

17. What can be learnt from the Synoptic Gospels about the cost of being a disciple of Jesus? Why does Jesus use a child as an example for his disciples to follow? 12,8

18. According to Mark's Gospel, what did James and John ask Jesus to do when he came into his glory, and what was Jesus' reply? What did Jesus teach about humility? 10,10

19. What do the Gospels teach about discipleship? 20

20. Describe three incidents in which Peter, James and John were specially chosen to accompany Jesus. 7,7,6

21. Describe three incidents in which Peter played an important part. What can be learnt about his character from these incidents? 7,7,6

22. What can be learnt from the Gospels about **a** Judas Iscariot, **b** Thomas **c** Matthew and **d** Peter? 5,5,3,7

Section C

23. Look up the references to Peter in the index and write a description of his character.

24. What qualities would you have looked for in your disciples if you had been Jesus?

25. Why were the twelve disciples a surprising group of people for Jesus to choose?

The Teaching of Jesus

1. The Sermon on the Mount
Matthew 5–7

Matthew presents a collection of sayings of Jesus in one sermon. It is very unlikely that Jesus would have preached this all at once. Some scholars think that Matthew was drawing a parallel between Moses giving the law on Mount Sinai and Jesus giving the new law on the Mount.

Some of the teaching contained in the Sermon is so revolutionary that it must go back to Jesus himself. It would not have been invented by the Gospel writers. Various interpretations of the Sermon on the Mount have been put forward. Two of the most important are:

    a. Jesus was putting his teaching in an extreme form in order to make people think. Much of it would be very difficult to obey.

    b. The teaching in the Sermon on the Mount presents a set of ideals. It may be very difficult or even impossible to live by these rules but those who try will become the true followers of Jesus.

THE BEATITUDES
Matthew 5:3–11 (Some also in Luke 6:20–23)

The form 'Blessed are...' is also found in the Old Testament, especially in the Psalms. Jesus was describing the right way to live and giving a promise of what the Kingdom of Heaven will bring.

a verse 3: The Kingdom of Heaven belongs to the poor in spirit.

This could refer to those who are materially poor (as in Luke) or to those who realise that they are spiritually poor before God. This shows that values will be reversed in the Kingdom of Heaven.

b verse 4: Those who mourn shall be comforted.

This could refer to those who are sympathetic to the suffering of others.

c verse 5: The meek shall inherit the earth.

This is from Psalm 37:11.

d verse 6: Those who hunger and thirst for righteousness shall be satisfied.

Luke has 'hunger' meaning those who are literally without food.

e verse 7: The merciful shall obtain mercy.

f verse 8: The pure in heart shall see God.

This could be a distinction between those who are really pure and those who are only ritually pure. In Psalm 24:4 those with 'clean hands and a pure heart' can stand before God.

g verse 9: The peace-makers shall be called the Sons of God.

These are those who are not merely peaceful people but those who actively work to bring about peace.

h verse 10: The Kingdom of Heaven belongs to those who are persecuted for the sake of righteousness.

JESUS' ATTITUDE TO THE LAW

In Matthew 5:17–18 Jesus says that he has not come to abolish the law and the prophets but to fulfil them. However, he makes the Torah more radical and rejects some of the Oral Tradition.

a Attitude to the Torah

The Torah was the written law and consisted of the first five books of the Old Testament which the Jews believed had been given to Moses by God. Jesus quoted from the Torah on numerous occasions. He widens the law by comparing the Torah with his new teaching. He extends the law to include thoughts as well as actions. In the teaching on divorce he rejects the Torah. However he upholds the law by telling the lepers to show themselves to the priest (Mk 1:44; Lk 17:14–19).

b Attitude to the Oral Tradition (The Halakah)

This was the interpretation which the scribes put upon the Torah. It was not a rigid, clearly defined code. Jesus argues with many aspects of the accepted interpretation, especially the rules about the Sabbath, and those about ritual purity. In Mark 7:6–8 Jesus accused the Jewish leaders of obeying rules which were made by man and disobeying the commandments of God. In other words, looking for the letter of the law and not the spirit. The law of Corban was an example of this. Jesus' criticisms of the Oral Tradition are so radical that they are unlikely to have been invented by the Gospel writers.

THE NEW LAW
Matthew 5:21–48

a Murder
5:21–26

The Torah said that murder was wrong and should be punished but Jesus says that anyone who is angry with his brother should also be punished. Jesus also warns against insulting your brother by calling him a fool. It is better to apologise to your brother before you offer your sacrifice and to make friends with your accuser on your way to court.

b Adultery
5:27–30

Adultery was forbidden in the Ten Commandments but Jesus extended the law to cover thought as well as action. Looking at a woman lustfully was as wrong as committing adultery.

v29–30 are paralleled in Matthew 18:8–9 and Mark 9:43–48

It is better to be without your eye or your hand than to sin and be punished in Gehenna. This was a ravine outside Jerusalem where rubbish was burnt. The Jews thought of it as a symbol of future punishment.

c Divorce
5:31–32

The Jewish law allowed a man to divorce his wife for 'some indecency' (Deuteronomy 24:1) There were two schools of thought about what 'some indecency' was. Rabbi Shammai defined it as adultery whereas Rabbi Hillel taught that it referred to anything which incurred the husband's displeasure, and destroyed the happiness of the family. However Jesus goes against the Torah by saying that there should be no divorce, in Mk 10:2–12. In Matthew 5:32 Jesus makes an exception and allows divorce for unchastity. This is thought to have been a later addition by Matthew to make Jesus' teaching agree with that of Rabbi Shammai.

See also Chap. 10 for Jesus' answer to the Pharisees' question about divorce.

d Oaths
5:33–37

Jesus is not referring to legal oaths but to the oaths which people continually made in ordinary conversation, to prove that whay they said was true. Jesus expects his followers to tell the truth at all times. A simple 'Yes' or 'No' is all that is needed.

e Retribution
5:38–42; Luke 6:27–31

'An eye for an eye and a tooth for a tooth' (Exodus 21:24) was called the Lex Talionis. By the time of Jesus this was not taken literally but money was substituted instead. However Jesus taught that there should be no retaliation and that they should not resist one who is evil.

    i)   If someone hits you on the right cheek offer the left. A blow on the right cheek, with the back of the hand, was regarded as an insult.

    ii)   If someone sues you for your coat give him your cloak as well. Exodus 22:26 forbad a creditor to keep a debtor's cloak overnight.

    iii)   If someone forces you to go one mile, go two. A soldier had the right to force a civilian to carry his equipment for one mile. (This statement by Jesus goes against Zealot teaching.)

    iv)   Do not refuse someone who begs or wants to borrow from you.

f Love
4:43–48

The command to 'love your neighbour' is from Leviticus 19:18. 'Hate your enemy' is not a specific quotation from the Old Testament but it can be inferred from many passages. Jesus may be quoting a popular Jewish proverb. Jesus commands his followers to love their enemies and pray for their persecutors. In Leviticus 'neighbour' meant a fellow Jew but Jesus extended it to mean everyone. eg. the Parable of the Good Samaritan.

See also the Question about the Greatest Commandment, Chapter Ten.

RELIGIOUS DUTIES
6:1–18

a) Almsgiving
6:2–4

Almsgiving was necessary to support those who otherwise would have starved. For this reason it was an important religious duty. The reference to blowing a trumpet may be metaphorical or it may refer to the trumpets which were sounded at public fasts. Some of the Jewish leaders made a show of their religion so that they would be admired. They also wanted to impress God. Jesus tells his followers to give alms so secretly that their left hand does not realise what their right hand is doing. Their Father will reward them. Jesus is using ideas of his day when he speaks of reward. The thought of reward should not be the motive for kindness.

See below: The widow's coin.

b Prayer
6:5–15

Jesus criticises the hypocrites who pray so that they can be seen and admired. Prayers should be said in secret. God who sees in secret will reward them. Jesus gives the example of the Lord's Prayer.

See below for Jesus' teaching on prayer.

c Fasting
6:16–17

Public fasts were held in autumn to pray for rain. Strict Jews fasted on Mondays and Thursdays during the drought. In the Parable of the Pharisee and the Tax Collector, the Pharisee boasts that he fasts twice a week. It was common for some people to leave their hair and beards dishevelled and to whiten their faces so that people would see that they were fasting. Jesus says that when they fast they should anoint their heads and wash their faces. Anointing usually took place at feasts.

See also Chapter 10 for the dispute with the Jewish leaders about fasting.

d Wealth
6:19–24

Jesus says that they should not store up riches on earth because they will not last. 'Rust' probably means being eaten by mice. An 'evil eye' (v22–23) was a common Jewish expression for being a miser. Therefore to have a sound eye is to be generous. Mammon (v24) means property. A person cannot be the slave of both God and possessions.

See below for Jesus' teaching on wealth.

e Anxiety
6:25–34; Luke 12:22–31

The phrase should be 'make anxious efforts for' rather than to be anxious about. Since this seems to be a command not to work to earn money it must only apply to Jesus' disciples who should concentrate on following him. They should take their examples from the birds and the lilies.

f Judgement
7:1–6; Luke 6:37–38

Verses 2–3 are probably contemporary proverbs. A 'speck' was a piece of dried wood or straw. However the saying about pearls being given to pigs shows that the disciples must show some discrimination. 'What is holy' were words which were used in the Eucharist.

g Prayer
7:7–11; Luke 11:9–13

If a man will not give his son a stone when he asks for bread, or a serpent when he asks for fish, how much more will God give good things to those who pray to him. (Luke has egg and scorpion instead.)

h The golden rule
7:12; Luke 6:31

'So whatever you wish that men would do to you, do so to them; for this is the law and the prophets.'

In Luke this is coupled with the saying about loving enemies. It is another attempt to sum up the law in one sentence. (See The Greatest Commandment, Chapter Ten.)

i Warnings
7:13–23; Luke 13:23–24; 6:43–44

In Matthew there is a broad and a narrow gate. In Luke a crowd struggles to enter by a narrow door. The simile of the two ways was common in Jewish literature. Jesus gives warnings against false prophets.

j The Parable of the Wise and Foolish Builders
7:24–27

See Chapter Eight.
This parable ends the Sermon on the Mount.

2.   Jesus' teaching on Prayer

a.   JESUS' OWN EXAMPLE
Prayer was very important in the life of a Jew. Prayers were said three
times a day. The first was at dawn when the Shema was recited.
Grace was said before and after every meal. Jesus would have
observed the three times of prayer. It is unlikely that the early
Christians would have observed them if Jesus had not (Acts 3:1).
Grace was said before and after the Last Supper and at the meal at
Emmaus (Lk 24:30). In the Synoptic Gospels only two prayers of
Jesus are recorded in addition to the Lord's Prayer and the words from
the cross, Mt 11:25f and Mk 14:36f. However Jesus went against the
usual Jewish pattern of prayer:

   a. Some Rabbis taught that public prayer was most likely to be
       heard. They also composed prayers for people to use. However
       Jesus prayed alone and spent hours and even whole nights at
       prayer eg. Mk 1:35, Mk 6:46, Lk 6:12.
   b. Jewish prayers were in Hebrew but Jesus seems to have prayed in
       his own language, Aramaic, eg. the Lord's Prayer was given to the
       disciples in Aramaic.
   c. It is likely that Jesus prayed using words from the Psalms, eg. the
       prayers from the cross.
   d. He did not use many names for God but used the simple term
       'Abba' which was an everyday children's word for father.
   e. Jesus showed willingness to accept God's will (eg. Mk 14:36).
   f. He made prayers of intercession (prayers on behalf of other
       people). It was not usual for ordinary Jews to do this because their
       religious leaders prayed for them. (eg. Lk 22:31, Lk 23:34)

b.   JESUS' TEACHING
   a. Prayers are to be said in secret and not in public. (Mt 6:5–6)
   b. Prayers are to be short, not like Gentile prayers which try to
       impress God with many words. (Mt 6:7)
   c. There has to be a readiness to forgive. (Mt 5:44)

d. Prayers will be answered. (Mt 7:7–8)

c.   THE LORD'S PRAYER
Matthew 6:9–13; Luke 11:2–4

Luke and Matthew have different versions of this prayer. Luke is the shortest and the whole of it is included in Matthew's account. It is probably that Luke is the original form because it is unlikely that Luke would have missed out some of the prayer, but it is possible that Matthew's Church may have added to it to make it more liturgical.

The address 'Father' goes back to the Aramic word 'Abba' (explained above). The first two phrases 'hallowed (praised) be Thy name' and 'Thy Kingdom come' came from the prayer which was said at the end of the synagogue service. The 'bread' may refer to ordinary bread or to the 'bread of life'. (See below for Jesus' teaching on forgiveness.) There is no parallel in Jewish literature for 'lead us not into temptation'. Jewish prayers ended either with a formal phrase or they were left for people to make up and ending for themselves. It is possible that originally the Lord's Prayer had a free ending.

See also *The parable of the friend at midnight.*   Chapter Eight
        The parable of the unjust judge.   Chapter Eight
        The sermon on the Mount.   (see above)
        The garden of Gethsemane.   Chapter Eleven
        The words from the cross.   Chapter Eleven

3.   Jesus' Teaching on Forgiveness

The Scribes believed that God would not forgive sins unless sacrifices were made or that sin was redeemed by good works. There are only two occasions in the Gospels when Jesus explicitly forgave sin, Mk 2:1–12; Lk 7:36–50, but he spoke about forgiveness on many occasions.

When Peter asked how many times he should forgive his brother Jesus said seventy times seven (Mt 18:21–22). In Luke, he says if a man sins seven times in one day he should be forgiven seven times. The Rabbis' usual answer was that a man must forgive his brother three times but Jesus believes that you should always forgive.

Jesus also showed forgiveness by his actions:
a. He ate with tax collectors and sinners (eg. Mk 2:15–17).
b. Matthew, one of Jesus' disciples was a tax collector (Mt 9:9).
c. Jesus went to the home of Zacchaeus who was a tax-collector in Jericho (Lk 19:1–10).

d. According to Luke, Jesus forgave those who crucified him (Lk 23:34).

See also *Parables about forgiveness* (Chapter Eight).

4. Jesus' Teaching on Wealth

Jesus advised people to store treasure in heaven instead of on earth, Mt 6:19–21. 'Treasure in heaven' was a Rabbinic phrase. The danger of wealth is that it separates men from God, (Lk 16:13). Money takes the place of God. Jesus told the rich young ruler to sell all that he had and give it to the poor and then follow him (Lk 18:18–25). The expression about a camel passing through the eye of a needle is an exaggerated way of saying that it is almost impossible for a rich man to enter the Kingdom of God. (Mt 19:16–22, Mk 10:17–22; Lk 18:18–25). However it is only the followers of Jesus who are told to give away all their possessions, eg. Zacchaeus was only told to give away half of what he possessed (Lk 19:1–10). The incident of the widow offering money in the Temple treasury (Mk 12:41–44, Lk 21:1–4) was probably originally a parable which has been turned into an incident. 'The two copper coins' were the smallest in circulation. The woman was praised because she had given a greater percentage of her possessions than the wealthy Pharisees.

See also *the parables about wealth.* (Chapter Eight)

the Sermon on the Mount. see above

5. Jesus' teaching on Race

In the incident of the Samaritan woman at the well (Jhn 4:7–42) Jesus is shown as breaking down the barrier between the two races. It was unusual for a Jew to ask a Samaritan for a drink because if he used the same cup he would become ritually unclean. When Jesus was on his way to Jerusalem the Samaritans refused to give him shelter but Jesus would not allow the disciples to call down fire on them, (Lk 9:51–56). Jesus' ministry was limited to Israel and its borders. He told the disciples that they were not to go outside Israel (Mt 10:5). However he rejected the idea that God was going to call down vengeance on the Gentiles. In Luke 4:18–19 Jesus quotes Isaiah 61 but he misses out the plea for vengeance. In the Parable of the sheep and the goats, 'all nations' are gathered before the Son of Man, (Mt 25:32). In the story of the cleansing of the Temple Jesus says that the

Temple should be a place of prayer for all the nations, Mk 11:17. Jesus' attitude may be summed up in 'love your neighbour' (Lk 10:27). Jesus interpreted 'neighbour' to mean everyone, irrespective of their race.

See also *Parable of the Good Samaritan.* (Chapter Eight)

Miracles involving Gentiles. (Chapter Nine)

Samaritan woman at the well. (Chapter Thirteen)

6. Jesus' Teaching about the End of the World

There are two accounts of what was expected at the end of the world. These are called Apocalypses, (a literary form, popular at the time of Jesus, in which the authors revealed their visions of the future.)

MARK 13:1–37
(this is expanded in Mt 24:1–25:46)

This is a prophecy of the distress which will occur.

a. False prophets will appear. There will be wars, earthquakes and famines. Christians will be persecuted.

b. 'The desolating sacrilege' will be set up. This expression is from Daniel 11:31. It was usually interpreted as meaning a false Christ. The people must escape.

c. The sun and moon will be darkened and the stars fall, before the Son of Man comes in the clouds in glory with his angels to gather the chosen. No-one knows when this will happen.

LUKE 17:20–37
No-one knows when the end will come but it will come suddenly. This is described in metaphors eg. like lightning, like the flood, like the punishment of Sodom. People will be divided, of two men in a bed, one will be taken, the other left.

These two accounts have different themes. Mark stresses the signs which will lead up to the end, whereas Luke stresses its suddenness. Many scholars think that Luke has the original teaching. The early Christians expected the end to come very soon. When it did not, they concentrated on the signs which would lead up to the end.

See the Parables about judgement and the end of the world. (Chapter Eight)

Work Section

Section A

1. Why is the teaching contained in the Sermon on the Mount thought to go back to Jesus himself?
2. What interpretations of the Sermon on the Mount have been made?
3. What is the reward of the poor in spirit?
4. Who will inherit the earth?
5. What will be the reward of the pure in heart?
6. What does Jesus say about the Law in Matthew 5:17–20?
7. Explain the difference between the Torah and the Halakah.
8. What will be the punishment for calling your brother a fool?
9. Why should you make friends with your accuser on the way to court?
10. What extreme measures does Jesus advocate to prevent your body being thrown into hell?
11. What does Jesus say about divorce?
12. Why does Jesus say that they should not swear by heaven, earth, or their heads?
13. What does Jesus recommend instead of retribution?
14. How does God treat the just and unjust equally?
15. How is Jesus' command to 'love your neighbour' different from that found in the Old Testament?
16. Which religious duties are Jesus' followers to perform in secret and why?
17. Why is it foolish to store up treasure on earth?
18. What is 'treasure in heaven'?
19. Why should Jesus' disciples not be anxious about tomorrow?
20. Explain what Jesus meant by Matthew 7:3–5.
21. What does Matthew 7:7–12 teach about prayer?
22. What is Jesus' golden rule according to Matthew 7:12?
23. How will people recognise false prophets?
24. Which two prayers of Jesus (other than the Lord's Prayer) are recorded in the Synoptic Gospels?

25. How were Jesus' prayers different from Jewish prayers?
26. Compare the Lord's Prayer in Matthew and in Luke, and list the differences.
27. What did Jesus teach about forgiveness?
28. Describe the incident with the rich young ruler.
29. Relate the story of the widow's coin.
30. How did Jesus demonstrate that he was not a racialist?
31. What is an Apocalypse?
32. How do the accounts of the end of the world, in Mark and Luke, differ? How can this difference be explained?

Section B

33. What types of people are described as 'blessed' by Jesus in the Sermon on the Mount and how will they be rewarded? What does Jesus say in the Sermon on the Mount about love? 14,6

34. What did Jesus teach in the Sermon on the Mount and on other occasions about **a** almsgiving, **b** fasting and **c** divorce? 7,7,6

35. Jesus said that he had not come to abolish the law and the prophets but to fulfil them. Discuss this statement with reference to three examples from the Sermon on the Mount. 7,7,6

36. What advice does Jesus give in the Sermon on the Mount about violence? 20

37. What does Jesus say in the Sermon on the Mount about **a** treasure on earth, **b** anxiety, **c** judgement and **d** false prophets? 5,5,5,5

38. What did Jesus teach about prayer? Give two examples of his own use of prayer. 12, 4,4

39. What was Jesus' reply to the rich man's question, 'What must I do to inherit eternal life?' What did Jesus teach about the dangers of wealth? 8,12

40. Jesus was not a racialist. Illustrate the truth of this statement by examining Jesus's relationship with Samaritans and Gentiles in the Gospel accounts. 20

41. What did Jesus teach about the end of the world. Narrate a parable which he used to illustrate this teaching. 12,8

42. Describe Jesus' teaching on forgiveness. Show how he put his teaching into practice in his own life. 12,8

Section C

43. How can teaching which is impossible to live by still have some value?

44. How far can Jesus' teaching about non retaliation and loving your enemies be put into practice in the modern world?

45. There are Christians who oppose nuclear weapons, and Christians who accept their necessity. What arguments, based on the teaching of Jesus, could each offer to defend these views? Are there any other arguments which need to be taken into consideration?

46. Compile your own list of characteristics which should be 'blessed'.

47. What is the modern Christian attitude to divorce?

48. Can the Christian ideal of marriage be upheld in the modern world?

49. Is it foolish to store up treasure on earth?

50. What should be the Christian attitude to football pools, raffles, bingo etc?

51. How do charities such as Christian Aid and Oxfam put Jesus' teaching into practice?

52. What do you think will happen at the end of the world?

53. How should Christians today put Jesus' teaching about race into practice, especially in relation to apartheid in South Africa?

54. Suggestions for further reading are:

Naught for your comfort, Trevor Huddleston.
North and South, (The Brandt Report)
Spend, Spend, Spend, Vivien Nicholson.

Parables

About a third of Jesus' teaching is in the form of parables. A parable is a story, taken from everyday life, which illustrates some teaching. The meaning is not explained but is left for the listeners to work out for themselves. The parables have a Palestinian background and the original Aramaic can be traced behind the Greek translation. Therefore most scholars believe that the parables contained in the Gospels were actually told by Jesus. The early Christians added their own interpretations to the parables and altered some of them into allegories before they were written down, eg. The Sower (Mk 4:3–9, 13–20). An allegory is a story in which everything stands for something else. The story has to be decoded in order to understand its meaning. It is unlikely that Jesus intended his parables to be allegories because they make the stories unnecessarily complicated.

Why Jesus taught in parables

a. Parables are interesting to listen to. Jesus had to attract the attention of the people who were passing by. Short stories were (and still are!) more interesting than long sermons.

b. Jews were used to listening to parables because it was their traditional method of teaching. It would have been surprising if Jesus had not told parables.

c. Parables are easy to remember. People at the time of Jesus did not usually write things down but recited stories from generation to generation, with a high degree of accuracy.

d. People have to interpret parables for themselves. This gives them a deep significance. They are intended to produce a response and so often include the question, 'What do you think?' eg. The Parable of the Good Samaritan. (Lk 10:36)

e. In the Gospels Jesus gave a strange reason for speaking in parables: 'To you (the disciples) has been given the secret of the Kingdom of God but for those outside everything is in parables; so that they may indeed see but not perceive, and may indeed hear but not understand; lest they turn again and be forgiven (Mk 4:11–12)'

This is a strange purpose. Jesus appears to be saying that he is deliberately attempting to confuse people. (This is not the intention of most teachers; although you may think otherwise!) Various interpretations have been given for these verses:

   a. Verses 11–12 do not originally belong to the section Mark 4:1–34. They are not really about Jesus' parables but his teaching in general, ie. the secret of the Kingdom of God has been given to the disciples but those outside do not understand and repent because they do not recognise who Jesus is.

   b. The early Christians believed that it was God's plan for the Jews to reject Jesus so that his death and resurrection could unite all people with God. (see Romans chapter 11)

   c. The verses were added to explain why the early church's teaching was rejected by the Jews. (see Acts 13:44–52)

The parables can be divided into different sections according to their meanings, although some can be listed under more than one heading.

Section A Parables about the Kingdom of God

 1. The Sower. (Mt 13:3–8, 18–23; Mk 4:3–8, 13–20; Lk 8:5–8, 11–15)
 2. The growth of the seed. (Mk 4:26–29)
 3. The mustard seed. (Mt 13:31–32; Mk 4:30–32; Lk 13:18–19)
 4. The weeds and the wheat. (Mt 13:24–30, 36–43)
 5. The leaven. (Mt 13:33; Lk 13:20–21)
 6. The hidden treasure. (Mt 13:44)
 7. The pearl. (Mt 13:45–46)
 8. The net of fish. (Mt 13:47–50)
 9. The two sons. (Mt 21:28–32)
10. The wedding feast. (Mt 22:1–14; Lk 14:16–24)
11. The wise and foolish builders. (Mt 7:24–27; Lk 6:47–49)
12. The lamp under a bushel. (Mk 4:21–25; Mt 5:14–16; Lk 8:16)
13. Wineskins and patches. (Mk 2:21–22; Mt 9:16–17; Lk 5:36–38)
14. The labourers in the vineyard. (Mt 20:1–16)

Section B Parables about wealth and possessions

15. The rich fool. (Lk 12:13–21)
16. The rich man and Lazarus. (Lk 16:19–31)

N.B. The parable of the dishonest steward has sometimes been regarded as a parable about wealth, although it is listed below under parables about judgement.

Section C Parables about forgiveness

17. The lost sheep. (Mt 18:10–14; Lk 15:3–7)
18. The lost coin. (Lk 15:8–10)
19. The Prodigal Son. (Lk 15:11–32)
20. The unforgiving servant. (Mt 18:23–35)
21. The pharisee and the tax-collector. (Lk 18:9–14)
22. The two debtors. (Lk 7:41–43)

Section D Parables about judgement

23. The wise and foolish virgins. (Mt 25:1–13)
24. The talents. (Mt 25:14–30; Lk 19:11–27)
25. The sheep and the goats. (Mt 25:31–46)
26. The barren fig tree. (Lk 13:6–9)
27. The tenants in the vineyard. (Mk 12:1–12; Mt 21:33–44; Lk 20:9–16)
28. The faithful servant. (Mt 24:45–51; Lk 12:42–48)
29. The door-keeper. (Mk 13:32–37: Lk 12:35–38)
30. The dishonest steward. (Lk 16:1–13)

Section E Parables about prayer

31. The friend at midnight. (Lk 11:5–8)
32. The unjust judge. (Lk 18:1–8)

Section F Parable about race

33. The good Samaritan. (Lk 10:25–37)

Section G Parables which criticise the Jewish leaders

N.B. There are many parables which come under this heading, but they have all been mentioned under other sections. The most important are:

The Pharisee and the tax-collector. (Lk 18:9–14)
The lost sheep and the lost coin. (Lk 15:3–10)
The Prodigal Son. (Lk 15:11–32)
The tenants in the vineyard. (Mk 12:1–12; Mt 21:33–44; Lk 20:9–16)
The talents. (Mt 25:14–30)
The wedding feast. (Mt 22:1–14; Lk 14:16–24)

Section A Parables about the Kingdom of God

The Kingdom of God. (see Chapter One.)

1 The Parable of the sower
Mark 4:3–8, 13–20; Matthew 13:3–8, 18–23; Luke 8:5–8, 11–15

This story describes the traditional method of sowing in Palestine. The seed was scattered before the land was ploughed. Therefore, the earth which was used as a path, the weeds, and the rocky ground would later be ploughed up or covered.

Interpretations: a. The first part of the story is about the problems of the seed being sown but the last part has moved forward to the time of the harvest. Jesus remained confident that the Kingdom would come even though many people did not accept his teaching. He often compared the Kingdom with a harvest.

b. The Gospels include an allegorical interpretation of the parable. This is generally thought to have been added by the early Church.

The Seed = the word.
The birds = Satan.
The seed on rocky ground = the people who listen at first but cannot stand up to persecution.
The seed amongst weeds = the people who become too preoccupied with earthly possessions.
The seed on good soil = people who respond with different levels of success.

2 The growth of the seed
Mark 4:26–29

The seed grows in secret. The farmer merely sows the seed.

Interpretations: a. The Kingdom of God is like the seed. It develops secretly inside a person.

b. The Kingdom of God is like the process of growth. It is produced by God's energy at work in the world, even though it is not recognised.

3 The mustard seed
Mark 4:30–32; Matthew 13:31–32; Luke 13:18–19

The tiny mustard seed produces a shrub which is eight to ten feet high. Matthew and Luke are exaggerating when they say that it becomes a tree.

Interpretations: The Kingdom of God is not being compared with the mustard seed, but with the final results of growth when it becomes 'a tree which shelters the birds.' This was a common metaphor for a great Kingdom which protected its subjects. The Jews had expected the Messiah to come in an obvious and glorious way but instead Jesus had gathered a small band of simple and often disreputable people, but by God's miraculous power they would become the people of God.

4 The weeds and the wheat
Matthew 13:24–30, 36–43

This is a realistic farming story. Darnel (the weeds) was common in Palestine. It looked like wheat when it first started growing. It was usual for farmers to weed it out but, because it had been planted deliberately, there was so much that the farmer decided to leave it until harvest time when it could be tied into bundles and used to light ovens.

Interpretations a. The main point of the parable is to show that patience is necessary. It was not yet time to separate the sinners from the righteous. The time of the harvest would be decided by God.

b. Matthew includes an allegorical interpretation:
The Sower = The Son of Man.

The field = The world.
The good seed = the sons of the Kingdom.
The weeds = the sons of the devil.
The enemy = the devil.
The harvest = the final judgement.
The reapers = the angels.

This allegory contains many expressions which Jesus would not have used. It is thought to have been added to give a warning about the last judgement.

5 *The leaven*
Matthew 13:33; Luke 13:20–21

This is very similar to the parable of the mustard seed. The amounts are exaggerated. A housewife would not make bread using fifty pounds of flour. In Romans 11:16 'the dough' is used as a metaphor for the people of God.

Interpretations: a. The same as for the mustard seed. ie. by God's power the small band of disciples can be transformed just as a tiny amount of yeast can transform a huge amount of flour.
b. As the tiny amount of yeast transforms the dough, so a few followers of Jesus are changing the world.

6 *The hidden treasure*
Matthew 13:44

Buried jars containing jewels or coins were often discovered in Palestine because it was the safest way to hide possessions. A man was legally entitled to any treasure found on his land.
This has the same meaning as:

7 *The pearl*
Matthew 13:45–46

Pearls were highly prized. It was an especially valuable pearl which the merchant found.

Interpretations: a. Both parables stress the need for people to give up everything to follow Jesus.
b. The stress may instead be on the great joy which makes

everything else unimportant. The experience of the Kingdom is so overwhelming that it totally changes people's lives.

8 *The net of fish*
Matthew 13:47–50

The drag net was pulled between two boats or laid out by one boat and drawn by two ropes. Jews were forbidden to eat fish which did not have scales and fins, eg. eels (Leviticus 11:10). Therefore the catch had to be sorted.

Interpretations: a. The coming of the Kingdom is compared with sorting fish. It will separate the good from the bad.
b. The stress may be on the disciples being told to spread their net widely to include all people.

9 *The two sons*
Matthew 21:28–32

One son is asked to go to work in the vineyard. He refuses but later changes his mind. The other son promises to go but does not keep his promise.

Interpretations: a. In Mt 21:32 this parable is applied to John the Baptist. John was rejected by the religious leaders but accepted by the sinners.
b. It has a more general meaning in that it shows that the tax collectors and sinners will enter the Kingdom of God rather than the religious leaders. The tax collectors and sinners have disobeyed God but they have repented. The religious leaders mistakenly claim that they are doing God's will.

10 *The wedding feast*
Matthew 22:1–14; Luke 14:16–24

Jesus probably based this story on a well known Jewish story about a tax-collector who became wealthy and sent out invitations in the hope that the rich land-owners would accept him. They all declined the invitations and in his anger the tax-collector filled the places at his feast with beggars to show the land-owners that he could do without them.

Interpretations: The self-righteous are like the guests who have refused

God's invitation, therefore the sinners are invited in their place.

Luke has two sets of invitations a. into the streets and lanes of the city, (meaning the sinners) b. into the highways and hedges, (meaning the Gentiles).

N.B. Matthew 22:11–14 is a strange addition. A man invited in from the street could not be expected to have a wedding garment. This is thought to be a separate parable added by Matthew to argue against the conclusion that everyone would be accepted into the Kingdom no matter how they behaved.

11 The wise and foolish builders
Matthew 7:24–27; Luke 6:47–49

Only a foolish builder would construct a house without foundations which would not withstand the autumn rains and storms.

Interpretation: Whoever hears Jesus' words and accepts them will be saved. Those who do not accept his teaching have no firm basis for their lives.

12 The lamp under a bushel
Mark 4:21–25; Matthew 5:14–16; Luke 8:16

A lamp is not hidden under a bushel (a tub used to measure grain which had a volume of eight gallons or thirty six litres) but it is put in a place where it gives out light.

Interpretations: a. Matthew adds the interpretation 'let your light so shine before men that they may see your good works and give glory to your father who is in heaven'. This is an unlikely interpretation since Jesus warns people about being pious so that they can be admired. (Mt 6:1)

b. It is a criticism of those Jewish teachers who have hidden the Kingdom of God instead of revealing it to the people.

13 Patches and wineskins
Matthew 9:16–17; Mark 2:21–22; Luke 5:36–38

It is foolish to sew a patch of new (unshrunken) material on to an old garment or to put new, fermenting wine into skins which will not stretch.

Interpretation: A garment was a common symbol for the world. The Jewish religion was worn out and no longer worth patching because Jesus had arrived.

Wine was a common symbol for salvation. Jesus' teaching is not an attempt to reform Judaism but something totally new which could not be fitted into the old system.

14 The labourers in the vineyard
Matthew 20:1–16

The vineyard owner visits the market place five times during the day to hire labourers. The harvesting and pressing had to be finished before the rainy season and so with a good crop the work had to be done quickly. The usual day's wage was a denarius. The 'fair' wage agreed with the last four groups of labourers would have been expected to be a fraction of a denarius.

Interpretations: a. The parable does not display limitless generosity. The owner only pays the usual wage but he pities the men who would only receive part of a day's wage. The parable is set in a time when there was a lot of unemployment. This is the way God treats men, he is merciful and even gives places in his Kingdom to tax-collectors and sinners.

b. The last part of the parable is aimed at the Scribes and Pharisees who resent Jesus mixing with tax-collectors and sinners.

Section B Parables about wealth and possessions

15 The rich fool
Luke 12:13–21

A man asked Jesus to decide how his inheritance should be shared with his brother. Jesus did not give a direct answer but told this parable.

Interpretation: The man was a fool because he believed that his wealth gave him security for the future. However, wealth is not important in God's eyes. The man's death points to the coming judgement.

16 The rich man and Lazarus
Luke 16:19–31

This is based on a well known Jewish folk story. The name 'Lazarus' means 'God helps'. A man who was a cripple, suffering from skin disease and licked by the wild dogs would have been seen as being punished by God for his sins. The 'crumbs' under the table were pieces of bread which were dipped into the dish, used to wipe their hands on and then thrown on to the floor. Lazarus' place next to Abraham would have been a great surprise for the Jewish audience. The small request of the rich man for a drop of water shows how extreme his torment was.

Interpretation: The rich man's selfishness is punished. Lazarus' humility is rewarded. The parable is a warning to anyone who resembles the rich man and his brothers.

Section C Parables about Forgiveness

17 The lost sheep
Luke 15:3–7, Matthew 18:10–14

A hundred sheep was a medium sized flock. It was usual to count the sheep at night before they were put into the fold. (It would however have been unusual for him to leave the ninety nine by themselves.)

Interpretation: In Luke Jesus tells this parable in response to the Pharisees' question about why he mixes with sinners. The parable shows that God will rejoice at the final judgement when a sinner repents.
N.B. Shepherds were regarded as sinful by some pious Jews because they were suspected of taking their flocks into Gentile areas.

18 The lost coin
Luke 15:8–10

The ten coins would have been on the woman's head-dress. This was part of her dowry. She was forbidden to take it off even when she slept. Since she only had ten coins she must have been poor.

Interpretation: The same as for the lost sheep.

19 The prodigal son
Luke 15:11–32

The title of this parable is misleading because it is the father, not the son, who is the most important character. The youngest son was entitled to a third of the property (Deuteronomy 21:17). He was probably under eighteen since he was not married. Working with pigs was one of the lowest jobs that a Jew could do. It is significant that his father was watching for him and ran out to meet him. The gifts which he gave to his son indicated that he had been accepted back as a son and not a servant:
   a. a robe was a mark of honour.
   b. a ring (probably a signet ring) was a sign of authority.
   c. Shoes were a luxury not worn by slaves.
   d. meat was not usually eaten so the killing of the fatted calf meant a feast to celebrate an important event.

Interpretations: a. The parable describes the love and mercy of God who welcomes back repentant sinners.
   b. The elder brother represents the righteous who can not understand Jesus' association with sinners. Like the elder brother they are being asked to accept God's invitation to rejoice.

20 The unforgiving servant
Matthew 18:23–35

The amount of the first debt is exaggerated. It is equivalent to tens of millions of pounds. Jesus' audience would have laughed at the hugeness of the amount which is designed to contrast with small debt of the other servant. The Jewish law did not allow a wife to be sold so the story is set amongst Gentiles. Even if the servant and his family had been sold the debt could not have been paid.

Interpretation: This is a parable about the last judgement. If God has forgiven you so you must forgive others. If someone abuses God's forgiveness they will be punished.

21 The Pharisee and the tax collector
Luke 18:9–14

The Pharisee fasts twice a week, even though the law only demanded one fast a year (on the Day of Atonement). He pays tithes on everything, including produce such as corn and oil on which tithes had already been paid by the producers. Tax Collectors were shunned by respectable people. Jesus' audience would have been very shocked by this parable. This is the type of prayer that a smug Pharisee would have used. The tax collector was in a hopeless position because in order to repent he would have had to give up his job and pay back the money he had made with a fifth extra.

Interpretation: God welcomes despairing sinners and rejects the self-righteous who do not realise that they need to be forgiven.

22 The Two Debtors
Luke 7:41–43

This parable is told in response to an event which took place in the house of Simon the Pharisee. The woman (most likely a prostitute) kissed Jesus' feet, washed them with her tears and wiped them with her hair. (It was considered disgraceful for a woman to let down her hair in front of men.) Jesus told the parable to explain why he allowed such a woman to touch him.

Interpretation: Only those who have the greatest need to be forgiven can appreciate the full meaning of God's love.

Section D Parables about judgement

23 The wise and foolish virgins
Matthew 25:1–13

Some accounts of Palestinian weddings are similar to the description in this parable. The day was spent in celebrations and dancing. The wedding feast took place at night. Women went out to welcome the bridegroom with lights. The bridegroom was often delayed because agreement could not be reached about the presents to be given to the bride's relatives. The girls without spare oil are foolish because they did not think of the possibility of the bridegroom being late.

Interpretations: a. The early church interpreted the parable to be about the second coming of Jesus. They used it to warn Christians to be prepared. They made it into an allegory by saying that Jesus was the bridegroom, the foolish girls were the Jews and the wise girls were the Gentiles.

b. It is more likely that Jesus was warning that the crisis was already upon them. They had to be ready to accept God's message.

24 The talents
Matthew 25:14–30; Luke 19:11–27

Matthew probably has the earliest version of this parable. Luke adds the story about a noblemen going on a journey to claim a Kingdom. A deputation is sent to prevent this. However, the man returns as King and takes revenge on his enemies. This was probably originally a separate parable based on an actual event. In 4 B.C., after the death of Herod the Great, his son Archelaus went to Rome to be confirmed as ruler over Judea. A Jewish deputation was sent to prevent it, but Archelaus returned as ruler and had his revenge. The parable was a warning that the crisis was about to fall on them, just as suddenly as Archelaus had returned.

The stress in the Parable of the Talents is on the third servant who buries his talent. (In Luke he does not even take this precaution but merely wraps it in a cloth.)

Interpretations: a. The early Church interpreted this parable as being about the second coming of Christ. The time leading up to the second coming was one in which Christians would be tested. It is unlikely however that Jesus would compare himself with the master who is so hard that he reaps where he does not sow.

b. This parable is really a criticism of the self-righteous who had been given so much by God but had made little use of it. They would soon be called to give an account of themselves.

25 The sheep and the goats
Matthew 25:31–46

It was usual in Palestine to have mixed flocks of sheep and goats. They had to be separated at night because the sheep had to be kept safe but the goats were allowed to stay outside the fold. The sheep were the most valuable and their white colour symbolised righteousness.

Interpretation: This parable describes the Last Judgement. People will be judged on the acts of love which they have performed.

26 *The barren fig tree*
Luke 13:6–9

Fig trees were planted in vineyards and vegetable gardens. They absorbed a lot of moisture from the ground. It was not usual to manure a fig tree because they grew so easily.

Interpretation: God is so merciful that he will grant a reprieve even after sentence has been announced. However God's mercy cannot be given to those who do not repent.

27 *The tenants in the vineyard*
Mark 12:1–12; Matthew 21:33–44; Luke 20:9–16

This story may be based on an actual event. At the time of Jesus Zealots were stirring up the Galilean peasants to revolt against their foreign landlords.

Interpretations: a. The Gospel writers understood this as an allegory:
The vineyard = Israel.
The tenants = the self righteous.
The owner   = God.
Messengers = the prophets.
The son   = the Messiah.
'The others' = the Gentiles.

However, Jesus' audience would not have recognised the son as Messiah because they would not have expected the Messiah to be killed.

b. The parable really stresses the wickedness of the tenants who even go so far as to kill the owner's son. The self righteous are like the tenants because they have misused what God has given them. The vineyard (the Kingdom of God) will be given to others (the tax collectors and sinners).

28 The faithful servant
Matthew 24:45–51; Luke 12:42–48

The unexpected return of the master would reveal whether his servant had been trustworthy.

Interpretations: a. The early Church interpreted this as a parable about the return of Jesus and the last judgement.
b. Jesus' audience would have understood the term 'servant' to mean the self-righteous. The parable is a warning to them that they will soon have to give an account of their actions.

29 The door-keeper
Mark 13:32–37; Luke 12:35–38

The two Gospel accounts are different. In Mark the door-keeper (in Luke, all the servants) was told to be ready for the master returning from a long journey (in Luke, from a banquet). In Luke the master rewarded the watchful servants by waiting upon them.

Interpretations: a. The early Church understood the parable to be about waiting for the second coming.
b. It may have the same meaning as the parable of the wise and foolish virgins. Jesus may be warning his audience that the crucial moment has arrived when they should accept God's word.
c. It may be aimed at those people who are not ready for the Kingdom of God.

30 The dishonest steward
Luke 16:1–13

This was probably based on an actual event. Jesus' audience would have expected him to disapprove of the steward but instead he praised him for his readiness to act to save himself.

Interpretations: a. The steward takes decisive action to get himself out of trouble. Jesus' audience face a similar crisis because the Judgement is about to come.
b. Another interpretation might be to stress that people should be as careful about their religious life as they are with their worldly goods.

Section E Parables about prayer

31 The friend at midnight
Luke 11:5–18

It is a duty in the East to entertain a guest. The housewife baked the bread every morning but it would be known in the village who had bread left. The family slept in one room on mats on the floor, therefore opening the heavy bolt on the door would have woken the whole family.

Interpretations: a.   Luke puts the parable in the context of prayer and uses it to emphasise the need for persistence in prayer.

          b.   The parable may be intended to explain that however inconvenient it was, the friend would get up and give the bread because he would realise his duty to be hospitable. The meaning is that if a reluctant man would wake his family in order to do a favour, how much more readily will God help those in need.

32 The unjust judge
Luke 18:1–8

The widow's problem was probably an unpaid debt. Her debtor may have been someone who was rich and influential. Therefore her only weapon was persistence.

Interpretation: If the Judge, tired of the woman's nagging, eventually decides in her favour, how much more readily will God listen patiently to the needs of the poor.

Section F Parable about race

33 The Good Samaritan
Luke 10:25–37

This parable was told in answer to the question, 'who is my neighbour?'. Samaritans were hated by the Jews because they had intermarried with Gentiles, they had built a rival Temple on Mt. Gerizim, they often attacked Jews who were foolhardy enough to go through Samaria on their way from Galilee to Judea, and they served as auxiliaries in the Roman army. The story was possibly based on an actual incident. The seventeen mile journey from Jerusalem to Jericho was a lonely one on a road notorious for robbers. The priest and the levite would have been made ritually unclean if they had touched the man and he was dead. Jesus' audience would have been very shocked that a Samaritan was the one who helped.

Interpretation: Everyone is your neighbour irrespective of race, even those whom you think of as your worst enemies.

N.B. For further information about Samaritans see (Chapter One).

Work Section

Section A

1. What is a parable?
2. What is an allegory?
3. List the four types of ground in the parable of the sower? What happened to the seed in each case?
4. In the parable of the weeds and the wheat, what do the servants want to do when they discover the weeds? What are they told to do instead?
5. What is leaven?
6. In the parable of the wedding feast, list the guests' excuses **a** in Matthew and **b** in Luke.
7. In the parable of the labourers in the vineyard, why were some of the labourers angry?
8. Why was the rich fool foolish?
9. What happened to Lazarus and the rich man after their deaths?
10. List the similarities between the parables of the lost sheep and the lost coin.
11. Why was the eldest son, in the parable of the Prodigal Son, angry?
12. In the parable of the unforgiving servant, why was the servant, who had been forgiven, later punished?
13. Describe the prayers of the pharisee and the tax-collector in the Temple.
14. Relate the parable of the two debtors.
15. In the parable of the wise and foolish virgins what happened when the bridegroom arrived?
16. How much was each servant given in the parable of the talents and what did they do with it?
17. List the ways in which the sheep had helped the Son of Man.
18. What did the vine-dresser do to the barren fig tree?
19. How did the owner prepare the vineyard in the parable of the tenants in the vineyard?

20. In the parable of the dishonest steward, how did he consider earning a living and what did he do instead to prepare for the future?

21. What happened when the man's friend came to him for help at midnight?

22. Describe the parable of the unjust judge.

23. In the parable of the Good Samaritan how did the Samaritan help the wounded man?

Section B

24. Relate the parable of the sower. Explain its allegorical meaning. 10,10

25. What does the phrase 'the Kingdom of God' mean? Relate two parables which Jesus told to describe the Kingdom. 6,7,7

26. Why did Jesus tell parables? Give an account of the parable of the wedding feast. 10,10

27. Relate the explain the parable of the labourers in the vineyard. What advantages are offered by the method of teaching in parables? 12,8

28. Give an account of two parables dealing with wealth or possessions. What other teaching does Jesus give about wealth? 8,6,6

29. Describe two parables about forgiveness. How did Jesus show forgiveness in the way he lived? 10,5,5

30. Describe the characters of the three people in the Parable of the Prodigal Son. What does this parable mean? 5,5,5,5

31. Relate two parables which criticise the Jewish leaders. Why did Jesus call them hypocrites? 7,7,6

32. What did Jesus teach about the end of the world? What does the parable of the sheep and the Goats teach about the coming of the Son of Man? 12,8

33. Relate either the Parable of the Tenants in the Vineyard, or the Parable of the Weeds and the Wheat, and give its allegorical interpretation. 20

34. Relate two parables about prayer. What other teaching did Jesus give about prayer? 5,5,10

35. What was Jesus' reply to the question, 'And who is my neighbour?' Give accounts of two occasions when Jesus helped non Jews or Samaritans. 10,5,5

Section C

36. Read 2 Samuel 12:1–6 as an example of an Old Testament parable. Why was a parable a good way to show David that he had done wrong?

37. Is the Parable of the labourers in the vineyard relevant to industrial relationships today?

38. Write a modern parable about life in school. (The parable of the sower may give you some ideas.)

39. How are parables and fables different?

40. Parables are used by many religions, the following books contain a selection of stories from Hinduism, Buddhism, and Islam:

One Man and his Dog, Henry Lefever
Tales of the Dervishes, Idries Shah.
Thinkers of the East, Idries Shah.

41. Read *Animal Farm* by George Orwell for a modern example of an allegory.

42. Further information about the parables contained in the Gospels will be found in: *The Parables of the Kingdom,* C.H. Dodd.
The Parables of Jesus, Joachim Jeremias.

Miracles

1. Understanding the Miracles

People at the time the Gospels were written had great powers of imagination. They liked large numbers and unusual events. They were uncritical of such stories. Today people are more concerned with historical truth, so that the miracle stories have to be interpreted. For the early Church miracles were evidence that Jesus was the Son of God. There was a tendency to exaggerate numbers, eg. Mark 10:46 has one blind man whereas Matthew has two (Mt 20:30). Some of the miracles in the Gospels are similar to legends and Rabbinic stories, eg. there is an account of Vespasian healing a blind man using saliva and a myth in the cult of Dionysius describing water being turned into wine. Gentile miracle stories had a definite pattern: the seriousness of the illness was stressed, there was a description of the cure, proof was given that the cure had worked and the effect on the people who saw the miracle was recorded. Some of the miracles in the Gospels follow this pattern.

The miracle stories can be interpreted symbolically. Illness and physical handicap can be understood as symbols of spiritual need, eg. the blind man could not only see physical objects after being healed, but he could also see that Jesus was doing God's work. The miracles are evidence that the Kingdom of God has come, (Mt 11:4–5). In the Kingdom, people are made complete.

The miracle stories are such an integral part of the Gospels that Jesus must have performed miracles. The malicious accusation that Jesus exorcised demons with the help of Beelzebub (Mk 3:22) is not likely to have been invented by the Gospel writers. The accusation would not have been made if Jesus had been unable to exorcise demons. Many of the accusations that Jesus broke the Sabbath were because he had performed healing miracles. This was one of the accusations made at Jesus' trial.

Our understanding of illness today is different from that of the New Testament. Most illness has a physical cause and presents physical symptoms. At the time of Jesus the symptoms would have been recognised but the cause would not have been understood, hence evil spirits or sin were blamed. Some illness is caused by emotional problems. This may take the form of strange behaviour (mental illness) or physical symptoms (psychosomatic illness). Some of Jesus' miracles can be interpreted as the healing of psychosomatic illness, eg. the paralytic let down through the roof, where forgiveness of his sins releases the man's body from paralysis. Modern faith healers are able to help such people. In all illness the attitude of the patient will help or hinder recovery. Faith in the doctor or the medicine has a significant effect.

The miracle stories can be divided into two main sections:

    a. Healing miracles, including the casting out of demons and raising to life.

    b. Nature miracles which demonstrate Jesus' power over nature, eg. the sea, food, catches of fish.

A Summary of the miracle stories

Healing miracles
A Exorcisms

1. The man with the unclean spirit. (Mk 1:21–18; Lk 4:31–37)
2. Legion. (Mt 8:28–34; Mk 5:1–20; Lk 8:26–39)
3. The Syrophoenician woman's daughter. (Mt 15:21–28; Mk 7:24–30)
4. The epileptic boy (Mt 17:14–20; Mk 9:14–29; Lk 9:37–43)
5. The blind and dumb demoniac. (Mt 12:22–23; Lk 11:14–23)
6. The dumb demoniac. (Mt 9:32–34)

B Miracles performed on the Sabbath

7. Peter's mother-in law. (Mt 8:14–17; Mk 1:29–31; Lk 4:38–39)
8. The man with the withered hand. (Mt 12:9–14; Mk 3:1–6; Lk 6:6–11)
9. The crippled woman. (Lk 13;10–17)
10. The paralysed man by the sheepgate. (Jhn 5:1–18)
11. The man born blind. (Jhn 9:1–41)
12. The man with dropsy. (Lk 14:1–6)
    See also The man with the unclean spirit. (1.)

C Miracles involving faith

13. The paralysed man let down through the roof. (Mt 9:1–8; Mk 2:1–12; Lk 5:17–26)

14. The woman with haemorrhages. (Mt 9:20–22, Mk 5:25–34; Lk 8:43–48)
15. Bartimaeus. (Mk 10:46–52; Lk 18:35–43; Mt 20:29–34)
16. The centurion's servant. (Mt 8:5–13; Lk 7:1–10)
17. Two blind men. (Mt 9:27–31)
18. The ten lepers. (Lk 17:11–19)
    See also The Syrophoenician woman's daughter. (3)
             The epileptic boy. (4)

D Raising to life miracles

19. Jairus' daughter. (Mt 9:18–19, 23–26; Mk 5:22–24, 35–43; Lk 8:41–42, 49–56)
20. The widow of Nain's son. (Lk 7:11–17)
21. Lazarus. (Jhn 11:1–44)

E Other healings

22. The leper (Mt 8:1–4; Mk 1:40–45; Lk 5:12–15)
23. The deaf and dumb man. (Mk 7:31–37)
24. The blind man. (Mk 8:22–26)
25. The official's son. (Jhn 4:46–54)

F Healings involving Gentiles

These have all been mentioned under other headings:
Legion. (2)
The syrophoenician woman's daughter. (3)
The centurion's servant. (16)
The ten lepers. (18)
The official's son. (25)

B. Nature miracles

26. The stilling of the storm. (Mt 8:23–27; Mk 4:35–41; Lk 8:22–25)
27. Walking on the water. (Mt 14:22–27; Mk 6:45–52; Jhn 6:16–21)
28. The feeding of the five thousand. (Mt 14:13–21; Mk 6:30–44; Lk 9:10–17; Jhn 6:1–14)
29. The feeding of the four thousand. (Mt 15:32–38; Mk 8:1–10)
30. The fig tree. (Mt 21:18–22; Mk 11:12–14, 20–22)

31. The tax money (Mt 17:24–27)
32. The catch of fish. (Lk 5:1–11; Jhn 21:1–14)
33. Water into Wine. (Jhn 2:1–11)

2. Healing miracles

A. EXORCISMS

At the time of Jesus illnesses were thought to be caused by demons. Therefore Jesus' healing miracles as well as exorcisms were seen as victories over Satan. Casting out demons is described in terms of battles between Jesus and the devil, eg. Mk 1:23–28. Jesus sent his disciples out to proclaim the Kingdom of God and to have power over evil. Satan is described as falling like lightning from heaven, Lk 10:18. There are no parallels to this in Jewish literature.

1. The Man with the Unclean Spirit
Mark 1:23–28; Luke 4:33–37

The powers of evil are described as recognising the authority of Jesus, and realising that he has come to destroy them and set up the Kingdom of God. The words used in v25 for 'rebuked' and 'be silent' were both used as ancient formulas for exorcism. The word translated as 'unclean' may mean evil.

2. Legion
Matthew 8:28–34; Mark 5:1–20; Luke 8:26–39

It is not certain where this event occurred because Gerasa is over thirty miles from the Sea of Galilee, and Gadara is six miles from the sea. Gergesa cannot be identified. It was a Gentile area. Tombs were thought to be favourite places for demons. The word used for 'legion' can either mean legion or a legionary. Therefore the man's reply might have been that he was a soldier because there were many like him. The description of the spirits entering the pigs would have been seen as proof that the man was really cured. However verses Mk 5:12–13 may have been from a popular Jewish story about an exorcism which had taken place in a heathen area. Two thousand pigs is an unusually large herd. A Roman legion had about six thousand men but a battalion had two thousand and forty eight.

N.B. Matthew has two demoniacs.

3. The Syrophoenician woman's daughter
Matthew 15:21–28; Mark 7:24–30

The emphasis in this story is on the conversation between Jesus and the woman, and not on the healing, even though it is done from a distance. 'Dogs' was a common description of Gentiles. Jesus is described as seeing his power as Messiah as being only for the Jews. The woman's daughter is cured not because of the woman's clever answer but because she showed faith in Jesus. This story may have been omitted by Luke because he did not want to offend his Gentile readers.

4. The epileptic boy
Matthew 17:14–20; Mark 9:14–29; Luke 9:37–43

The description of the boy's illness is that of epilepsy. The disciples have been unable to cure the boy. The father says that he has faith but not enough. The miracle demonstrates the power of faith and the need for prayer.

5. The blind and dumb demoniac
Matthew 12:22–23; Luke 11:14–23

Matthew and Luke substituted this story for Mark 3:20–21 in order to give a suitable introduction to the accusation that Jesus was possessed by Beelzebub.

6. The dumb demoniac
Matthew 9:32–34

This is similar to the account of Matthew 12:22–23

B. MIRACLES PERFORMED ON THE SABBATH
See Chapter Ten for further discussion about the disputes with the Jewish leaders concerning miracles performed on the Sabbath.

7. Peter's mother-in-law
Matthew 8:14–17; Mark 1:29–31; Luke 4:38–39

It is possible that Mark 1:16–39 may come from Peter himself as it contains insignificant details and the stories seem to have been changed from the first to the third person. The comment that the woman prepared their meal demonstrates how completely she was cured.

8. The man with the withered hand
Matthew 12:9–14; Mark 3:1–6; Luke 6:6–11

As the man was not in danger of death Jesus was breaking the Sabbath laws by healing him. Jesus defends breaking the laws when good can be done.

9. The crippled woman
Luke 13:10–17

The woman is described as being crippled by a spirit. Jesus uses the image of releasing an ox or an ass for water to show that the woman should be released from Satan's power. The crowd rejoiced at the miracle but the Jewish leaders could not see the significance of Jesus's actions.

10. The paralysed man by the sheepgate
John 5:1–18

There was an underground stream under the pool which disturbed the water occasionally. The people believed that this was done by an angel and that the first one to enter the pool would be cured. The man was accused of breaking the Sabbath laws by carrying his pallet. Jesus' defence was that God would not rest on the Sabbath from his work of sustaining the universe. The man does not accept responsibility for getting into the water or carrying his bed. Jesus warns him to beware lest something worse happens to him.

11. The man born blind
John 9:1–41

The question of whose sins caused illnesses was a common theological problem at the time of Jesus. The water used at the Feast of Tabernacles was taken from the pool of Siloam. Verses 8–34 are like a trial of Jesus. The man who was cured pointed out that a sinner could not perform such a miracle.

12. The man with dropsy
Luke 14:1–6

Jesus is in the house of a leading Pharisee. The main meal was taken after the morning synagogue service. Dropsy is swelling caused by excess fluid in the blood.

C. MIRACLES INVOLVING FAITH

13. The paralysed man
Matthew 9:1–8; Mark 2:1–12; Luke 5:17–26

It is possible that the story may originally have consisted of v1–5 and 11–12. Verses 3–4 are vivid details which suggest a real event. Palestinian houses had steps on the outside. Roofs were made from wattle and daub. The dispute with the Jewish leaders was probably added to the story to show that Jesus' claim that he could forgive sins was not blasphemous. Even in the Old Testament the Messiah was not expected to forgive sins. Jesus heals the man because of the faith of his friends. This story demonstrates the Jewish belief that illness was caused by sin.

14. The woman with haemorrhages
Matthew 9:20–22; Mark 5:25–34; Luke 8:43–48

The woman was not able to approach Jesus openly because she was ceremonially unclean. She probably suffered from a continuous menstrual flow, (Leviticus 15:25–30). Matthew and Luke say she touched the fringe, the sacred part of Jesus' robe. However the story stresses that it is the woman's faith which has cured her and not the magic of the robe. The belief that cures could be made by touching people was common at the time of Jesus, see Acts 5:15. Jesus is shown to be in full control of his power.

15. Bartimaeus
Mark 10:46–52, Luke 18:35–43; Matthew 20:29–34

This account contains the first public and unrebuked recognition of Jesus as Messiah. Jesus acknowledges the title 'Son of David' by performing the miracle. The incident may be to contrast the faith of the blind man with the disciples, who although they can see, are blind to who Jesus is. Only Mark includes the name Bartimaeus, which means son of Timaeus. A beggar would have removed his cloak to spread it on the ground to collect money in. This story may have been used by the early Church as a model of encouragement. People are blind until Jesus opens their eyes.

16. The centurion's servant
Matthew 8:5–13; Luke 7:1–10

In Matthew's account the centurion approaches Jesus himself, but in Luke the Jewish elders ask Jesus to help the centurion because he had built their synagogue. This may mean that he was a proselyte, but in that case Jesus would not have been defiled by entering his house.

There are certain difficulties in the story. In Mt 8:7 Jesus says that he will come and heal him, but in v8 the centurion refuses to let him. The centurion's comment that he is under authority does not really make sense when he goes on to explain his ability to command soldiers. It is possible that v7 is in fact to be read as Jesus asking whether he should come (into a Gentile house) and heal the servant. Jesus may therefore be refusing as he did at first in the story of the Syrophoenician woman's daughter. However the centurion has enough faith to believe that Jesus can heal the servant without entering his house. In the same way that he can give orders to his soldiers, so Jesus can control the evil spirit which is possessing his servant. Luke stresses that the faith of the centurion is greater than that shown by the Jews.

17. The two blind men
Matthew 9:27–31

This may be the same story as Bartimaeus. It is also similar to Mark 8:22–26 when Jesus touched the blind man's eyes.

18. The ten lepers
Luke 17:11–19

This incident may be based on the healing of the leper in Mk 1:40–45. Jesus was on the border of Samaria on his way to Jerusalem. The lepers stood at a distance because they were forbidden to approach people. Jesus told the lepers to show themselves to the priest. Leviticus 14 describes the sacrifices and rituals which had to be performed before the priest could give a leper a certificate to say that he was clean. Jesus praises the Samaritan who is the only one to return to thank him.

See also the healing of the leper, (22)

D.   RAISING TO LIFE MIRACLES

19. Jairus' daughter
Matthew 9:18–19, 23–26; Mark 5:22–24, 35–43, Luke 8:41–42, 49–56

The term used for 'ruler of the synagogue' can also mean any religious leader, or prominent member of the synagogue. Only Matthew mentions the flute-players who were an important part of Jewish mourning. Sleep was a common way of talking about death at the time of Jesus. Christians also used 'sleeping' because they believed that one day everyone would be raised. The story contains many details which are typical of such stories in the ancient world: Jesus took her by the hand, the witnesses were astonished, the girl needed food (ghosts do not). Some ancient wonder workers used formulas in a foreign language and it was believed that these would lose their power if they were translated. This may be why Mark includes the Aramaic words 'Talitha Cumi.'

20. The widow of Nain's son
Luke 7:11–17

This story is very similar to the raising of a young bride by Apollonius of Tyana in 1 A.D. The bereaved widow would be destitute because the boy was her only son. Jesus felt sorry for her. The bier was a long wicker basket on which the body was laid. The words in v15 are similar to 1 Kings 17:23 when Elijah raised a widow's son.

21. Lazarus
John 11:1–44

Martha and Mary have not been mentioned in John's Gospel before this incident but they are in Luke 10:38. Lazarus had been dead for four days. The Jews believed that after the third day the soul ceased to hover over the body and death was complete. Jesus is described as being 'deeply moved'. This phrase usually expresses anger rather than grief. He may have been angered by the lack of faith in the resurrection of the mourners.

This story is very difficult to understand. It may be possible to suggest that in the other two accounts of Jesus raising people to life, they were not dead but in a coma. It is unlikely that John created the story out of nothing yet it is unusual that such a significant incident should have been missed out by the writers of the Synoptic Gospels.

E.   OTHER HEALINGS

22. The leper
Matthew 8:1–4; Mark 1:40–45; Luke 5:12–15

Leprosy involved ritual uncleanness and complete segregation. The law could not heal the leper and so it protected the rest of the community. According to the Rabbis the healing of leprosy was as difficult as raising the dead. Any skin disease was described as 'leprosy' at the time of Jesus.

Jesus broke the law by touching the man, probably to give him confidence. However Jesus upheld the law by ordering the man to show himself to the priest. Leviticus 14 describes the ritual washing and shaving and the sacrifices which had to be made before a man could be certified as clean.

23. The deaf and dumb man
Mark 7:31–37

In this healing Jesus:

   i. puts his fingers in the man's ears.

  ii. puts saliva on the man's tongue.

 iii. looks up to heaven.

 iv. uses the Aramaic word 'Ephaphtha' which means 'be opened'.

These details are similar to the techniques used by healers at the time of Jesus.

24. The blind man
Mark 8:22–26

This is very different from the healing of Bartimaeus. The miracle is performed in secret, saliva is used and the cure is gradual. Matthew and Luke may have missed this story out because it might be thought to indicate that Jesus lacked power. There is a similar story of a blind man being cured at Epidaurus. The first things he saw were the trees in the Temple precincts.

25. The official's son
John 4:46–54

This story may be based on the centurion's servant. The Greek word for son can also be translated as 'servant'. The officer was probably in the service of Herod Antipas.

F   NATURE MIRACLES

These accounts are the hardest to understand. It is possible to find explanations for healings and exorcisms because they occur today but it is difficult to understand power over the sea etc. The stories may be historically true or they may be symbolic stories which demonstrate that Jesus really was the Messiah.

26. The stilling of the storm
Matthew 8:23–27; Mark 4:36–41; Luke 8:22–25

This story would have been important in the early Church because it gives an assurance that Christians could have complete confidence in Jesus in times of trouble. Storms were common metaphors for evil forces and especially the troubles which the righteous faced. The ability to control the sea was an example of God's power (eg. Psalm 89:8–9). Jesus is described as being asleep with his head on a cushion. This was probably the wooden or leather seat used by the helmsman. In the Old Testament the ability to sleep peacefully was seen as a sign of perfect trust in God. Sudden storms were frequent on the Sea of Galilee. The disciples interpreted Jesus' sleep as a sign that he did not care. 'Peace be still' is better translated as 'be muzzled'. The words may have been used by wonder workers at the time of Jesus.

27. Walking on the water
Matthew 14:22–27; Mark 6:45–52; John 6:16–21

This story may have grown out of the stilling of the storm. The phrase 'on the sea' may mean 'on the sea shore'. Jesus may have walked to the boat through shallow water. The story encourages early Christians to maintain their faith in Jesus during times of trouble. It is possible that this may be a resurrection appearance which has been put in earlier by the Gospel writers.

Luke may have missed this story out because it is similar to pagan stories.

28. The Feeding of the five thousand
Matthew 14:13–21; Mark 6:30–44; Luke 9:10–17; John 6:1–14

This is the only miracle which is in all four Gospels. Attempts have been made to rationalise the story, but there is no real evidence to support any conclusion:

a. The numbers may have been exaggerated.
b. The disciples may have shared their food and the people followed their example.
c. It may have been a eucharistic meal at which everyone received a fragment of food.
d. Jesus may have filled people with 'spiritual food' ie. his teaching.

However it is more likely that the story has a symbolic meaning:

a. It is an anticipation of the Messianic banquet which was to take place in the Kingdom of God. Jesus acts in the same way as a host entertaining guests. The host usually took the bread, blessed it and broke it and began by eating some. When there were many people present, servants distributed the food.

b. It may be an anticipation of the Eucharist. Early Christians sat in orderly rows whilst the deacons brought the bread which had been blessed and broken.

c. Jesus is providing food as God had provided manna in the wilderness. John 6:4, 'Now the Passover, the feast of the Jews was at hand,' points to this understanding. The prophet Elisha had performed a similar miracle (2 Kings 4:42–44). Jesus is fulfilling the law and the Prophets.

Five thousand people and five loaves may represent the five books of the Torah. The twelve baskets of left over scraps probably represents the twelve tribes of Israel. The baskets referred to were the large wicker baskets used by farmers.

29. *The feeding of the four thousand*
Matthew 15:32–38; Mark 8:1–10

This story is so similar to the feeding of the five thousand that it is probably another version of the same incident. There is no reason why Jesus could not have repeated the miracle but the disciples would have not been so surprised the second time. It is possible that the story was so important for the early Church that it was often repeated and changes were made.

It has been suggested that the feeding of the five thousand represents the feeding of the Jews and the four thousand the feeding of the Gentiles. The seven loaves and seven baskets may be symbols of the seventy nations of the Gentile world, the seven deacons in Acts, the Septuagint, or the mission of the seventy. The word used for basket in this story is that carried by fishermen.

30. *The fig tree*
Matthew 21:18–22, Mark 11:12–24

This is a very difficult incident to understand. The fig tree was cursed because it did not have any fruit on it, but it would have been strange if it had since it was Spring. This action was irrational and out of character for Jesus. One explanation is that it is a prophetic action. Old Testament prophets often acted out their prophecies, eg. Jeremiah broke an earthenware flask (Jeremiah 19:1–13). The fig tree is like the self-righteous who make an outward show of their religion but produce no real fruits of righteousness, and like the fig tree the self-righteous will be condemned. It is also possible that the story was originally a parable (see Luke 13:6–9) and it has been turned into a miracle story. Jesus may have said that the end was so near that no one would eat the fruit from that tree again.

31. The tax money
Matthew 17:24–27

The tax was half a shekel which was paid every year to the Temple by all male Jews over the age of nineteen. It was collected in March. Various explanations have been given for this miracle:

a. Jesus may have told Peter to cast his hook into the sea and sell the fish which he caught to pay the tax.

b. The story may be based on popular Jewish legends about precious objects being found in the mouths of fish.

The story was probably written to demonstrate that Jesus paid the Temple tax. Jesus does things which the Son of God might not be expected to do, but the problem is solved by God providing the money. However Jesus' action could not be used to say that Christians should pay the tax.

(See also the question about taxes to Caesar in chapter ten.)

32. The Catch of Fish
Luke 5:1–11 (See also John 21:1–14, Chapter 13)

This may be a symbolic description of the saying about being fishers of men.

33. Water into wine
John 2:1–11

In the East wine was a symbol of a new age. The six stone jars each contained about twenty gallons of water, which was used for ritual washing. The story demonstrates Jesus' ability to change lives as dramatically as the water becomes wine. The exaggerated amount of wine emphasises this ability.

Work Section

Section A

1. What is the difference between a healing miracle and a nature miracle?
2. What is an exorcism?
3. What did the man with the unclean spirit in the synagogue cry out?
4. Describe the life which Legion led before he met Jesus.
5. Why were the people from the town afraid when they saw Legion?
6. What did Jesus tell Legion to do?
7. Where was Jesus when he met the Syrophoenician woman?
8. Why did Jesus refuse at first to heal her daughter?
9. What was the woman's reply?
10. What event immediately preceded the healing of the epileptic boy?
11. Describe the symptoms of the epileptic boy.
13. What happened to the boy?
14. Why could the disciples not cast the spirit out?
15. How long had the woman in the synagogue been possessed by a 'spirit of infirmity'?
16. For how many years had the man by the Sheep Gate been paralysed?
17. Why had the man not been cured?
18. Describe what happened after he had been cured.
19. How did Jesus cure the blind man in John 9:1–41?
20. What did Jesus say to the lawyers and Pharisees after he had cured the man with dropsy?
21. Where was Jesus when he cured the paralysed man let down through the roof?
22. What did Jesus say to the paralysed man which angered the scribes?
23. How long had the woman with haemorrhages suffered from her flow of blood?

24. How had she tried to find a cure?
25. What did Jesus say which surprised the disciples?
26. What did the blind man at Jericho cry out?
27. Where was Jesus when he cured the centurion's servant?
28. What was wrong with the servant?
29. What did Jesus say about the faith of the centurion?
30. What did the ten lepers ask Jesus?
31. What did Jesus tell them to do?
32. What message did Jairus receive when Jesus was on his way to the house?
33. Which disciples witnessed the raising of Jairus' daughter?
34. Why did the people laugh at Jesus?
35. How old was the girl?
36. How did Jesus cure her?
37. What instructions did Jesus give to the girl's parents?
38. How did Jesus raise the widow of Nain's son?
39. How did the crowd react when they witnessed this miracle?
40. Where did Lazarus and his sisters live?
41. What message did the sisters send to Jesus and what was his reply?
42. What did Martha say when Jesus arrived?
43. What happened when Jesus saw Mary weeping?
44. Why was Martha reluctant to roll the stone from the tomb?
45. What happened when Jesus shouted 'Lazarus come out'?
46. What did the leper ask Jesus to do?
47. How did Jesus cure the leper and what instructions did Jesus give to him?
48. Where was Jesus when he cured the deaf and dumb man?
49. Describe the healing of the blind man at Bethsaida. (Mk 8:22–26)
50. How did Jesus calm the storm?
51. Why were the disciples filled with awe?
52. Why were the disciples terrified when they saw Jesus walking on the water?
53. What did Jesus say to them?
54. What happened when Jesus got into the boat with them?
55. Before the feeding of the five thousand why did Jesus have compassion on the crowd?
56. What did the disciples tell Jesus to do when it grew late?
57. Why were the disciples surprised when Jesus told them to feed the crowd?

58. According to Mark's Gospel, how did the crowd sit?
59. In the feeding of the four thousand, how long had the crowd been with Jesus?
60. In the miracle of the tax money, what did Peter catch, and how was he to use it?
61. Where did Jesus perform the miracle of turning water into wine?
62. Why did Jesus refuse to help at first?
63. What did the steward tell the bridegroom after he had tasted the wine?

Section B

64. Describe **a** an exorcism, **b** a nature miracle, **c** a healing and **d** a raising to life, performed by Jesus. 5,5,5,5

65. Give an account of three miracles which were performed on the Sabbath. 6,7,7

66. Compare and contrast the healing of Legion with that of the epileptic boy. 20

67. Describe three occasions on which Jesus helped Samaritans or Gentiles. 7,7,6

68. Relate one miracle in which the faith of the sick person, and one in which the faith of the person's friends, was important. 10,10

69. Give an account of the raising of Lazarus. What problems are raised by this story? 15,5

70. Describe two occasions on which Jesus cured leprosy. Why was leprosy treated so seriously at the time of Jesus? What guidelines did the Jewish law lay down about the disease? 5,5,5,5

71. Compare and contrast the healing of the blind man at Bethsaida with that of the blind man at Jericho. How can this type of miracle be understood symbolically? 14,6

72. Briefly describe the healing of Jairus' daughter as recorded by Mark and the healing of the paralysed man at the Sheep Gate in John's Gospel. What discussion followed the healing of the paralysed man? 7,7,6

73. Give an account of the first miracle that Jesus performed in Cana in Galilee. What lesson do you think that the author of the fourth Gospel intended his readers to draw from it? 14,6

74. Describe two nature miracles and explain why nature miracles are more difficult to believe than healing miracles. 7,7,6

75. Give an account of the feeding of the five thousand according to Mark's Gospel. What differences are found in John's account? How can this miracle be interpreted? 8,4,8

76. How does our understanding of illness today differ from that at the time when the Gospels were written? Briefly describe three miracles which illustrate this difference. 8,4,4,4

Section C

77. Are Jesus' miracles really an acceptance of the temptation in the wilderness to do tricks in order to attract attention?

78. Do you think that the work of faith healers today is evidence for the truth of the Gospel healings?

79. Why do you think that people at the time of Jesus thought that mental illness was caused by demon possession? Do people still believe in demon possession today?

80. The feeding of the five thousand can be interpreted as a miracle in which people shared their own food. How could we recreate the miracle today?

Disputes with the Jewish leaders

See Chapter One for notes on the Pharisees, Scribes, Sadducees and Herodians.

This chapter summarises the Gospel accounts of conflicts between Jesus and some of the Jewish leaders. It is important to remember that the Gospels contain the beliefs of first century Christians and therefore the attitude towards Jews which they express is not necessarily the same as Christians would hold today. Christianity had broken away from Judaism and by the time the Gospels were written the majority of Christians came from Gentile backgrounds. It was believed that Jesus had come from God and he had tried to reform Judaism but that his ideas were rejected by the leaders of the Jews. Therefore in the Gospels it was inevitable that Jesus would come into conflict with some of the leading Jews. He disagreed with the emphasis which they placed on the Oral Tradition, and especially on the ritual law. He accused them of being so concerned with petty details that they missed the most important part of the law. According to the Gospels the Jewish leaders were trying to do God's will but they thought that their piety made them superior to other people. They did not believe that Jesus came from God because he broke the Oral Tradition, consequently he deserved punishment. On several occasions the stories of the disputes with representatives of the Jews end with them plotting to have Jesus killed.

Listed below are the Gospel accounts of disputes. The Revised Standard Translation has been used. It is important to remember that the picture which emerges from these stories of the Jewish leaders is not a complete picture. The accusations would be true of some scribes but not of all. In the same way today it would be possible to show that the Church had rejected the teaching and standards of Jesus by carefully selecting a set of stories which give evidence for that claim, e.g. Jesus taught that divorce was wrong but many churches permit divorced people to remarry in church.

1. Arguments about the Sabbath

N.B. Further information about the miracles performed on the Sabbath will be found in Chapter Nine.

Jesus' attitude to the Sabbath is summed up in Mark 2:27,
'The Sabbath was made for man, not man for the Sabbath.'

He rejected the Oral Tradition which listed actions which were not allowed on the Sabbath. The only thing which could justify breaking the Sabbath laws was danger to life. This exception was introduced during the battles of the Maccabean period to allow Jewish soldiers to fight on the Sabbath. Jesus rejects the Oral Tradition because it puts petty rules above love. Under the Oral Tradition Jesus deserved death by stoning for deliberately breaking the Sabbath.

a) Plucking Corn
Matthew. 12:1–8; Mark 2:23–28; Luke 6:1–5.

Accusers: Pharisees

Accusation: Jesus' disciples were plucking corn as they walked through the fields. The Law allowed a traveller to eat ripe grain, which had fallen (Deuteronomy 23:25). However the Scribes regarded plucking corn as reaping which was one of the thirty-nine activities forbidden on the Sabbath, (Exodus 34:21).

Jesus' Reply: Jesus uses a Rabbinic method of argument by referring to an Old Testament story. The Jews regarded David as their greatest king, but he had broken the Law when it was necessary for the sake of his men. Jesus concluded that the Sabbath was made for man and not man for the Sabbath. The only parallel to this idea is when Rabbi Simeon defined the Sabbath as 'a blessing and a gift to men.' (Mishna)

v28. 'The Son of Man is Lord even of the Sabbath,' was probably added by Mark. It implies that Jesus had a special right to break the Sabbath, whereas by using the story of David, Jesus had been trying to show that any human need was more important than Sabbath laws.

b) The Man with the Withered Arm
Matthew 12:9–14; Mark 3:1–6; Luke 6:6–11.

Accusers:	Pharisees
Accusation:	Jesus was about to break the Sabbath by curing a man with a withered arm. Healing was only allowed on the Sabbath when life was in danger.
Jesus' Reply:	Jesus asks them if it is permitted to do good or harm, to save life or to kill, on the Sabbath. In Matthew Jesus refers to the concession which the Scribes made that a sheep could be rescued from a pit on the Sabbath.

N.B. Mark 3:6 states that the Pharisees and Herodians discussed how to destroy Jesus. According to contemporary Jewish law a death sentence could only be pronounced if the accused had been warned in front of witnesses and if it had been made certain that he had acted deliberately. The incident of plucking corn fulfilled these two considerations. Therefore the next time Jesus broke the Sabbath (the withered arm incident according to Mark) left him open to being brought to judgement.

c) The Man with Dropsy
Luke 14:1–6

Accusers:	Lawyers and Pharisees
Accusation:	Jesus was about to break the Sabbath by healing a man with dropsy.
Jesus' Reply:	Jesus heals the man and asks if one of them had an ass or an ox which fell into a well on the Sabbath, would they not pull it out?

d) The Crippled Woman
Luke 13:10–17.

Accuser:	The ruler of the Synagogue.
Accusation:	Jesus had healed a woman who had been bent over for eighteen years. The ruler said that there were six days on which to heal people but not the Sabbath.

Jesus' Reply: It is hypocritical to untie an ass or an ox and take it out to drink on the Sabbath but not to free the woman who had been bound by Satan for eighteen years.

  e) The Man by the Pool of Bethzatha
  John 5:1–18

Accusers: The Jews
Accusation: Jesus had healed the cripple on the Sabbath. The cured man was also breaking the Sabbath by carrying his bed.
Jesus' Reply: 'My Father is working still, and I am working.'

  f) The Blind Man
  John 9:1–41

Accusers: Pharisees
Accusation: Jesus had broken the Sabbath by curing a man who had been born blind.

John does not record a reply by Jesus but has a conversation between the Pharisees and the man who had been healed.

Other miracles performed on the Sabbath are:

The Man with the Unclean Spirit. Mk 1:21–28, Lk 4:33–37.
Simon's Mother in Law. Mt 8:14–15; Mk 1:29–31; Lk 4:38–39.

2   Eating with Sinners
  Matthew 9:9–13; Mark 2:13–17; Luke 5:27–32

Accusers: Scribes and Pharisees
Accusation: By eating with sinners and tax collectors Jesus was:

  a   eating food on which tithes may not have been paid.
  b   being defiled by touching dishes which were unclean.
  c   associating with people who would be shunned by pious Jews.

Jesus' Reply: The healthy do not need a doctor but the sick do. Jesus has come for sinners and not for the righteous.

Eating with others had a special significance for Jews. It was a sharing of trust and brotherhood and also of the blessing which came from the breaking of bread. Jesus not only accepted the honour of being invited by Pharisees, (eg. Luke 14:1–6) but he also ate with sinners.

3   Fasting
Matthew 9:14–17; Mark 2:18–21; Luke 5:33–39

Accusers: In Mark and Luke, the people.
            In Matthew, John's disciples.

Accusation: Why do John's disciples and the disciples of the Pharisees fast but Jesus' disciples do not?

Jesus' Reply: The bridegroom's friends do not fast whilst the bridegroom is with them. Jews were exempted from fasting at weddings. Jesus is comparing himself with the bridegroom. Fasting may be suitable in preparation for the coming of the Kingdom but now it is as out of place as fasting at a wedding.

4   Eating with Defiled Hands
Matthew 15:1–20; Mark 7:1–13

Accusers: Pharisees, and some Scribes from Jerusalem

Accusation: Some of Jesus' disciples were eating without ritually cleaning their hands.
            This ritual washing was originally only a duty for priests when they ate the tithes and the offerings of fruit. The Pharisees obeyed this regulation even though they were not priests. Mark's phrase that all the Jews obeyed this rule is not strictly correct. It had become widely accepted by all Jews by 100 A.D. so that when Mark wrote the Gospel many Jews would have obeyed this law.

Jesus' Reply: a. Jesus uses a quotation from Isaiah (29:13) which accuses the people of honouring God with their lips but not with their hearts and teaching their own laws instead of God's. Jesus accuses the Pharisees of following their oral tradition at the expense of the written law.

            b. Jesus uses the Law of Corban to prove that the Jews broke the Law in order to keep the Oral Tradition.

'Corban' means 'a gift devoted to God'. The Law of Corban made it possible for a son to dedicate his money to the Temple instead of supporting his parents as the Torah demanded. However it was possible for him to keep the money for himself.

c. The food which a person eats cannot defile him because it passes out of the body. A person is defiled by his evil thoughts and actions.

5 Healing by the Devil
Matthew 12:22–37, 43–45; Mark 3:22–30; Luke 11:14–23

Accusers:	Mark, Scribes
	Luke, some people
	Matthew, Pharisees
Accusation:	Jesus was possessed by Beelzebub (the Prince of Devils) who enabled him to cast out devils.
Jesus' Reply:	It is illogical for Satan to cast out Satan. If a Kingdom is divided against itself it cannot survive. No one can break into a strong man's house and steal his property unless he ties the strong man up first. Whoever slanders the Holy Spirit can never be forgiven. (This may be the sin of calling good evil.)
	In Luke Jesus asks who their people cast out devils by if he is doing it with the help of the devil.

6 A Question about Divorce
Matthew 19:3–9; Mark 10:2–12

Questioners:	Pharisees
Question:	'Is it lawful for a man to divorce his wife?'
	(Matthew adds '. . . for any cause'.)
	The Jewish Law said that a man could divorce his wife if he found 'some indecency' in her (Deuteronomy 24:1–4). There were two schools of thought about what 'some indecency' meant:
	a. Rabbi Shammai said that it meant adultery.

b. Rabbi Hillel said that it could mean anything, e.g. even, in some circumstances, burning the dinner.

Jesus' Reply: Jesus argues that the law of divorce was only given as a concession to human weakness. God's real intention was that at marriage the two people became one flesh (Genesis 2:24). Man cannot separate what God has joined together. Jesus is therefore disagreeing with the Torah.

Mk 10:11–12, anyone who marries a divorced person commits adultery.

In Matthew Jesus says that there could be no divorce except for unchastity. By adding this Matthew has made Jesus agree with Rabbi Shammai. However it is likely that Mark has the original teaching because it is more strict.

N.B. More information about Jesus' attitude to divorce will be found in the Sermon on the Mount, Chapter 7.

The following four questions were asked in Jerusalem during the last week of Jesus' life in an attempt by the Jewish leaders to trick him into giving grounds on which to charge him.

7 A Question about Jesus' Authority
Matthew 21:23–27; Mark 11:27–33; Luke 20:1–8

Questioners: Chief priests, scribes and elders
ie. representatives of the Sanhedrin

Question: 'By what authority are you doing these things...?

Jesus' Reply: Jesus uses a Rabbinic method of debate by replying with a question: 'was the baptism of John from heaven or from men?'

The questioners were in difficulty because if they said that John was an ordinary man, they would be unpopular with the crowd who believed that John had been a prophet sent by God. If they said that he was from God then Jesus could ask them why they had not listened to him. Since they could not commit themselves to either view they were unable to answer his question. Jesus refused to answer their question.

Jesus' question is not an evasion. He is indicating that his authority is based on what happened when he was baptised by John.

8   A Question about Tax
Matthew 22:15–22; Mark 12:13–17; Luke 20:20–26

Questioners: Pharisees and Herodians

Question: 'Is it lawful to pay taxes to Caesar or not?'
This was the poll tax which had been introduced in A.D. 6. (See the Zealots, Chapter One). It was very unpopular because it reminded the Jews of Roman rule. The silver coins had the head and inscription of the Emperor Tiberius. The question was a trap because if Jesus had said that they ought to pay the tax he would be unpopular with the nationalist groups. However if he said that they should not pay them he could be arrested by the Romans.

Jesus' Reply: He asked for a silver coin and inquired whose head and inscription was on it. According to ancient ideas, coins were the property of the ruler who issued them. Jesus said that they should pay to Caesar what belonged to Caesar and to God what belonged to God. Jesus could be regarded as agreeing with both the Herodians, who supported paying taxes to Caesar and the Pharisees who supported giving taxes to the Temple.

Jesus may have believed that the Kingdom of God was imminent and that the future of the Roman Empire was short. Man's duty to the State should not conflict with his duty to God.

9   A Question about Resurrection
Matthew 22:23–33; Mark 12:18–27; Luke 20:27–40

Questioners: Sadducees

Question: There were seven brothers. The first married and died childless. The second married the widow and also died childless. Eventually all the brothers married her and died without children. Finally the woman also died. Whose wife will she be at the resurrection?

The Sadducees did not believe that there was anything in the Law about resurrection. They argued that the rule of Levirate marriage was incompatible with resurrection. This rule stated that when a man died without children his brother had to marry the widow. The rules in Deuteronomy (25:5–10) were designed to keep property in the family. Levirate marriage was not usual at the time of Jesus.

Jesus' Reply: a. When people rise they will be like angels and therefore it is ridiculous to think that they will marry.

b. The Sadducees are mistaken in thinking that there is no resurrection because it is implied in the Torah. When God appears to Moses at the burning bush he says he is the God of Abraham, Isaac and Jacob. All these were dead but the story records God speaking in the present tense. The conclusion is that they still exist.

10   A Question about the Greatest Commandment
Matthew 22:34–40; Mark 12:28–34; Luke 10:25–37.

Questioner: A Scribe

Question: 'Which commandment is the first of all?'

Many Rabbis had attempted to sum up the Law in one phrase. Rabbi Hillel (20 B.C.) said 'Do not to another what seems to you to be hurtful; that is the whole Torah. All the rest is commentary. Go and learn.'

Jesus' Reply: a. 'Hear, O Israel: The Lord our God, the Lord is one; and you shall love the Lord your God with all your heart, and with all your soul, and with all your mind, and with all your strength.' This is the beginning of the Shema (Deuteronomy 6:4–5) which every pious Jew recited daily.

b. 'You shall love your neighbour as yourself.' This is from Leviticus 19:18 where 'neighbour' meant 'fellow-country-man'. However Jesus used 'neighbour' to refer to anyone. This is explained in Luke's Gospel in the Parable of the Good Samaritan.

In Mark, this scribe agreed with Jesus that these laws were more important than sacrificial offerings. Jesus said that he was not far away from the Kingdom of God.

Jesus' Warnings about the Scribes and Pharisees

In the time of Jesus there was a distinction between Scribes and Pharisees but this is not apparent in some parts of the New Testament. Matthew speaks of Jesus addressing both the Scribes and the Pharisees at the same time so that the distinction between the two groups disappears. This reflects Matthew's own time since the Pharasaic Scribes had become the dominant group after A.D. 70. However, the parallel passage in Luke enables us to separate which criticisms were aimed at the Scribes and which the Pharisees.

Jesus' main charge against both the Scribes and the Pharisees is that they are hypocrites. The word originated in the Greek theatre and meant a 'play actor', i.e. someone who appears to be what he is not. Jesus tells the people to do what the Scribes and Pharisees tell them but not to follow their practice because they say one thing and do another. (Mt. 23:1–3)

1. JESUS' CRITICISMS OF THE SCRIBES

    a) They walk about in long robes.
    Mark 12:38; Luke 20:46

This probably refers to the Jewish shawl called a Tallith. These were to be worn at times of prayer and when performing other scribal duties. However they wore them continually to demonstrate their piety.
Mt. 23:5 refers to the deep fringes which they wore on these garments.

    b) They wear broad Phylacteries.
    Matthew 23:5

These were the leather boxes containing passages from the Torah. They were tied to the hand and forehead.

    c) They enjoy being greeted respectfully in the street.
    Matthew 23:7; Mark 12:38; Luke 20:46

The rule was that a man should acknowledge his superior in knowledge of the Law. Some distinguished Rabbis waived this right.

d) They want the places of honour at feasts.
Matthew 23:6; Mark 12:39; Luke 20:46

In the time of Jesus seating at feasts was determined by learning.

e) They want the chief seats in the synagogues.
Matthew 23:6; Mark 12:39; Luke 20:46, 11:43

These seats were on the platform facing the congregation.

f) They devour the property of widows
Matthew 23:14; Mark 12:40; Luke 20:47

This possibly refers to the large sums which a few scribes charged for making long prayers on behalf of widows. However, this was not true of most scribes who were good men.

g) They like to be addressed as 'Rabbi'.
Matthew 23:7–12

This was a term of respect used by scholars to their teachers. Jesus says that they have only one Rabbi and one Father. The greatest must become a servant. Whoever exalts himself will be humbled and he who humbles himself will be exalted.

h) They have taken away the key of knowledge. They did not enter the Kingdom of God Themselves and prevent others from entering.
Luke 11:52; Matthew 23:13

i) They load intolerable burdens onto the backs of others and yet do not lift a finger to help.
Matthew 23:4; Luke 11:45–46

The driver of a beast of burden would ease its load by removing some of the weight which it carried but the scribes would not ease the burden which their rules imposed.

j) They decorate the tombs of the prophets and claim that they would not have murdered them if they had been alive at the time of their ancestors. Jesus says that they share the guilt of their fathers for all the blood shed from the time of Abel to Zechariah, that is, throughout all Jewish history.
Matthew 23:29–36; Luke 11:47–51

2. JESUS' CRITICISMS OF THE PHARISEES

a) They are like cups which are clean on the outside but inside are full of greed and wickedness.
Matthew 23:25–26; Luke 11:37–41
They are like white-washed tombs.
Matthew 23:27–28; Luke 11:44
Graves were marked before festivals to prevent pilgrims from accidentally touching a tomb and thus becoming ritually unclean. Both these two criticisms mean that on the outside the Pharisees might appear to be pious but inside they are full of evil.

b) They travel over land and sea to make one convert and when they have found him they make him twice as fit for hell as themselves.
Matthew 23:1

Converts to Judaism were divided into two classes. The Godfearers, who only obeyed the Sabbath and the food laws, and the Proselytes who accepted all the Jewish regulations. The Pharisees were eager for Godfearers to become proselytes.

c) Jesus says they pay tithes on herbs like dill, mint and cummin but they have neglected the weightier demands of the law.
Matthew 23:23; Luke 11:42

In Leviticus and Deuteronomy Jews were commanded to pay tithes on 'the seed of the land', and 'the fruit of the tree' and on 'corn, wine and oil'. The Pharisees extended this to include even tiny herbs.

d) They strain out a gnat but swallow a camel.
Matthew 23:24

This refers to their practice of straining wine in order to remove dead insects. If these were swallowed the Pharisees would become ritually unclean.
Both these last two criticisms show Jesus' opposition to petty laws which make people blind to God's real demands. There was a Jewish saying, 'he that kills a flea on the sabbath is as guilty as if he killed a camel.'

e) They are blind guides because of their teaching about oaths.
Matthew 23:16–22

They had a rule that if a man took an oath by the Temple or the Altar he was not bound by it. However if he swore by the gold which was in the Temple and the offering which was on the Altar then he was bound by it. Jesus argues that without the Temple the gold is not important and without the Altar the offering is meaningless.

Work Section

Section A

1. Why was it inevitable that Jesus would come into conflict with the Jewish leaders?
2. Where was Jesus when he cured the man with the withered arm?
3. What was Jesus' reply to the accusation that his disciples had broken the law by plucking corn on the Sabbath?
4. Who plotted to destroy Jesus after this event?
5. Where was Jesus when he cured the man with dropsy?
6. Why was the paralysed man lying by the Sheep Gate?
7. What happened after the paralysed man had been cured?
8. How did Jesus cure the blind man in John 9:1–41?
9. Describe the conversation which took place after this healing?
10. What information does Mark 7:3–4 give about the customs of the Pharisees?
11. Compare and explain Jesus' teaching on divorce in Matthew and in Mark.
12. How was the question about the payment of taxes to Caesar a trap?
13. Explain Jesus' reply to the Sadducees question about resurrection?
14. List the questions which Jesus answered in the Temple.

Section B

15. Who were the Pharisees? Describe two incidents in which they played an important part. 6, 7, 7.
16. Describe three occasions on which Jesus was accused of breaking the Sabbath. What was Jesus' reply to these accusations? 7, 7, 6.
17. How did Jesus reply to the accusation that his disciples ate with unclean hands? Briefly describe an occasion when the Pharisees and Herodians tried to catch him out. 12, 8.
18. Why did the leaders of the Jews want to destroy Jesus? Describe two occasions when they tried to trap him. 8, 6, 6.

19. Describe three occasions when Jesus was accused of breaking the ritual law. How did Jesus justify his actions? 7, 7, 6.

20. Who were (a) the scribes and (b) the Pharisees? What criticisms did Jesus make of each group? 5, 5, 5, 5.

21. What did Jesus teach about (a) divorce, and (b) attitude to women, according to the Gospels? How did his teaching differ from that of the Jewish leaders? 7, 7, 6.

22. What discussions did Jesus have in the Temple with the Pharisees and Herodians, the representatives of the Sanhedrin, and the Sadducees? 7, 6, 7.

23. What was Jesus' answer to the question 'Which commandment is the first of all?' How did Jesus further illustrate his answer according to Luke's Gospel? 8, 12.

Section C

24. What sort of person would be described as being 'like a Pharisee' today?

25. Why are the Gospels hostile to the Jews?

The Death of Jesus

1. Jesus' Predictions of his death

The Synoptic Gospels record three distinct predictions which Jesus made about his death, on the way to Jerusalem. It has been suggested that these were made up after the resurrection and put into the mouth of Jesus by the Gospel writers. This may be true of certain details, but Jesus would have realised that his teaching would result in his death, and would probably have given warnings to his disciples. There are also many other occasions when Jesus spoke indirectly about his coming sufferings, eg. after the Transfiguration.

Jesus was constantly in conflict with the Jewish leaders and broke rules, eg. the Sabbath laws, for which the penalty was death. He was warned about breaking the Sabbath after the incident about plucking corn and under Jewish law once a warning had been given, punishment could be inflicted for a second offence.

The predictions contain some details which were not fulfilled. There are hints that Jesus expected death by stoning (Lk 13:34), violence after his death, (Lk 22:35–38), and suffering for the disciples (Mk 14:27).

The First Prediction
Matthew 16:21–23; Mark 8:31–33; Luke 9:21–22

After Peter's confession that Jesus was the Messiah, Jesus warned the disciples not to tell anyone. He would be rejected by the Jewish leaders, and be killed, but he would rise on the third day. The phrase 'the third day' means 'a short time'. Semetic languages did not have a word for 'few' but used 'three' instead. Peter told Jesus that this could not happen. Jesus saw this as another temptation not to suffer, and he addressed Peter as 'Satan' telling him that he thought as men thought, not as God.

The Second Prediction
Matthew 17:22–23; Mark 9:30–32; Luke 9:43–45

Jesus gave the second prediction during a secret teaching expedition in Galilee.

a. The Son of Man will be delivered up.

b. He will be killed.

c. After three days he will rise again.

The disciples again did not understand what he was saying.

N.B. Luke does not include points b. and c.

The Third Prediction
Matthew 20:17–19; Mark 10:32–34; Luke 18:31–34

Jesus gave this more detailed prediction as he approached Jerusalem. The six stages of Jesus' way to the cross are listed. Many scholars think that this list was composed after the events.

a. The Son of Man will be delivered up to the chief priests and scribes.

b. He will be condemned to death.

c. He will be handed over to the Gentiles.

d. He will be mocked, spat upon and scourged.

e. He will be killed.

f. After three days he will rise.

2. The last week of Jesus' life

Mark arranged the events leading up to the Crucifixion chronologically to form one week. This is an artificial arrangement since the events in Jerusalem probably took longer than a week. According to Mark, Jesus taught in the Temple for two days and yet when Jesus was about to be arrested he asked why they had not arrested him in the Temple since he had taught there 'day by day'. Matthew and Luke copy Mark's material. The only major difference is that Matthew inserts several parables. John has a much shorter account and does not give Jesus' teaching in the Temple in detail. Mark probably arranged the events to form a week because the early Church was already celebrating Holy Week and it gave a structure for their worship.

Sunday: The entry into Jerusalem. (Mt, Mk, Lk, Jhn)

Monday: The cursing of the fig tree. (Mt, Mk)
The cleansing of the Temple. (Mt, Mk, Lk, John has this event at the beginning of Jesus' ministry.)

Tuesday:	Teaching in the Temple:

a. The question about authority. (Mt, Mk, Lk)
b. The parable of the tenants in the Vineyard. (Mt, Mk, Lk)
c. The parable of the Marriage feast. (Mt)
d. The question about taxes to Caesar. (Mt, Mk, Lk)
e. The question about resurrection. (Mt, Mk, Lk)
f. The question about the greatest commandment. (Mt, Mk, Luke has this earlier in Jesus' ministry.)
g. Warnings about the scribes and pharisees. (Mt, Mk, Lk)
h. The widow's coin. (Mt, Mk, Lk)
i. Predictions about the end of the world. (Mt, Mk, Lk)
j. The parable of the wise and foolish virgins. (Mt)
k. The parable of the talents. (Mt)
l. The parable of the sheep and the goats. (Mt)

Wednesday:
a. The betrayal plot. (Mt, Mk, Lk)
b. The anointing in Bethany. (Mt, Mk, Luke has this earlier in Jesus' ministry; John has it before the entry into Jerusalem.)

Thursday:
a. Preparation for the Passover. (Mt, Mk, Lk)
b. The Last Supper. (Mt, Mk, Lk, Jhn)
c. The prediction of Peter's denial. (Mt, Mk, Lk, Jhn)
d. The arrest in the garden of Gethsemane. (Mt, Mk, Lk, Jhn)
e. The trial before the council. (Mt, Mk, Lk, Jhn)
f. Peter's denial (Mt, Mk, Lk, Jhn)

Friday:
a. The trial before Pilate. (Mt, Mk, Lk, Jhn)
b. The trial before Herod. (Lk)
c. The scourging. (Mt, Mk, Lk, Jhn)
d. The crucifixion. (Mt, Mk, Lk, Jhn)
e. The burial. (Mt, Mk, Lk, Jhn)

3. The entry into Jerusalem
Matthew 21:1–9; Mark 11:1–11; Luke 19:29–38; John 12:12–15

Jesus is described as acting out the prophecy from Zechariah 9:9, in order to declare that he is the Messiah:

'Rejoice greatly O daughter of Zion.
Sing aloud, O daughter of Jerusalem!
Lo your King comes to you;
triumphant and victorious is he,
humble and riding on an ass.'

This prophecy is specifically mentioned in Matthew (21:5) and in John (12:15) but it is implied in Mark and Luke. The significance of Jesus riding from the Mount of Olives is from Zechariah 14:4. Pilgrims usually entered Jerusalem on foot. The usual interpretation is to say that Jesus was stressing that he was not a military Messiah. However, it has been questioned whether the Zechariah prophecy would have been interpreted at the time as depicting a peaceful Messiah.

It is strange that such a clear demonstration of Jesus' Messiahship did not produce more reaction from the people or the authorities. Some scholars have suggested that Jesus rode into Jerusalem at the time of the Feast of Dedication, which commemorated the cleansing of the Temple by Judas Maccabeus in 165 B.C. During this celebration branches were waved and Psalm 118 was chanted. The entry of Jesus may have been part of this celebration and the words chanted may therefore not have been to welcome Jesus as Messiah.

Mark stresses the miraculous nature of the story. However Jesus may have had a prearranged plan to borrow the colt. It was customary to welcome an important person by spreading clothes and fragrant herbs on the ground. In its original context Psalm 118, which contains the words:

'Hosanna! Blessed is he who comes in the name of the Lord.'
merely invoked a blessing on pilgrims on their way to Jerusalem for a festival.

4. The cursing of the fig tree
Matthew 21:19–22; Mark 11:12–14, 20–25

(See Chapter 9).

5. The cleansing of the Temple
Matthew 21:12–16; Mark 11:15–18; Luke 19:45–48; John 2:13–16

According to the Gospels Jesus entered the Temple and:
a. drove out those who bought and sold.
b. overturned the tables of the money-changers.

c. turned over the seats of the pigeon sellers.

d. forbad people to carry things through the Temple, using it as a short-cut.

Traders in the Court of the Gentiles (see the plan of the Temple on pg 18), sold wine, oil, salt, birds, and probably animals, to pilgrims for sacrifices. These had to be bought with Jewish or Phoenician money therefore Roman and Greek coins had to be changed. The trading may actually have been carried out by the priests themselves. The trading was legitimate and was for the benefit of pilgrims. Using the Temple as a short-cut was forbidden by the law. Jesus objected to the Court of the Gentiles being used as a market place instead of being a place where the Gentiles could pray. Jesus' words, 'Is it not written, "my house shall be called a house of prayer for all the nations"? But you have made it a den of robbers,' are a combination of Isaiah 56:7 and Jeremiah 7:11. Jesus' action also fulfills the prophecy of Malachi 3. John's Gospel puts this incident at the beginning of Jesus' ministry but it fits better at the end.

The story raises the problems of how one person could turn over the tables and drive people out and why Jesus was not arrested by the Temple police. It is possible that the story may have been exaggerated.

6. Teaching in the Temple

This teaching has been covered in other sections of the book:

see: Chapter Ten.

The question about authority.

The question about taxes to Caesar.

The question about resurrection.

The question about the greatest commandment.

Warnings about the Scribes and Pharisees.

see: Chapter Eight

The parable of the tenants in the vineyard.

The parable of the marriage feast.

The parable of the wise and foolish virgins.

The parable of the talents.

The parable of the sheep and the goats.

see: Chapter Seven

The widow's coin.

Predictions about the end of the world.

7. The betrayal plot
Matthew 26:1–5, 14–16; Mark 14:1–2, 10–11; Luke 22:1–6; John 11:47–53

Mark has the basic story. The other Gospel writers have added their own details, eg. Matthew mentions the amount of money agreed, thirty pieces of silver. The authorities realised that if Jesus was arrested openly it might cause trouble amongst the crowds. They wanted to avoid this by taking him secretly.

Various suggestions have been made about why Judas betrayed Jesus:
  a. He wanted the money. However he could probably have struck a better bargain. Thirty pieces of silver was equivalent to 120 denarii. (A denarius was the usual day's wage.)
  b. He was jealous of the other disciples, especially Peter, James, and John.
  c. He was frightened for his own safety and therefore changed sides to save himself.
  d. Luke and John say that Satan entered him.
  e. He might have expected Jesus to be a military Messiah and thought that by arranging for his arrest he would be put in a position where he would have to fight back and rally an army to defeat the Romans.

In Matthew 27:3–10, Judas repented and took the money back to the chief priests and elders. Since it was 'blood money' they used it to buy a field to bury strangers. Acts 1:16–20 records Judas' gory end:

'falling headlong, he burst open in the middle and all his bowels gushed out.'

8. The anointing in Bethany
Matthew 26:6–13; Mark 14:3–9; Luke 7:36–38; John 12:1–8

Mark and Matthew say that Jesus was in Bethany in the house of Simon the Leper. John says he was in the house of Martha and Mary. Luke has a slightly different story set at a different place in Jesus' ministry. (see the parable of the two debtors, Chapter 8.) Tradition says that the woman was Mary Magdalene although she is not named in the Gospels. The oil which she poured over Jesus' head (Luke and John have 'feet') was nard, which was from a rare Indian plant. Jesus contrasted the narrow attitude of those who criticised the woman with the generosity and love shown by her.

Anointing was used on various occasions:

a. In rich circles guests were anointed before a meal.

b. Kings were anointed at their coronation.

c. Bodies were anointed after death. Jesus is recorded as saying that the woman has anointed him in readiness for his death. Mark says that the woman broke the flask. This could be to show that she used all the oil, or to reinforce the anointing for death image because the flask was usually broken and the pieces put in the coffin.

d. The word 'Messiah' means 'anointed one'. The position of the story in Mark could be to demonstrate that although Jesus was hated by the Jewish authorities and was about to be betrayed by one of his own disciples, the woman was ready to recognise him as the Messiah.

9. Preparation for the Last Supper
Mark 14:12–16; Mathew 26:17–19; Luke 22:7–13

The dating is ambiguous and depends on whether the Last Supper was a Passover meal. Water jars were only carried by women, (men carried leather bottles.) Mark uses this story to demonstrate Jesus' supernatural powers (as in the story of the fetching of the colt). It could however have been a prearranged plan so that Jesus could eat the meal in secret without being arrested. There is a tradition that the room was in the house of the mother of John Mark (the author of Mark's Gospel) but there is no evidence to support this in the New Testament.

10. The Last Supper
Matthew 26:20–35; Mark 14:17–25; Luke 22:21–23; John 13–Ch. 17

There is much debate amongst scholars about whether this was a Passover meal. The Synoptics (using Mark as their source) describe it as such but John's Gospel has the crucifixion taking place on the day on which the sacrificial lambs were killed in preparation for the Passover. John therefore has the supper a day earlier.

Points in favour of a Passover (Seder) meal

a. John may have deliberately put the events a day earlier to stress the symbolism of Jesus as the sacrificial lamb.
b. Jesus' words over the bread and wine follow the pattern of the Passover meal when the head of the family had to explain the significance of the food and wine.
c. Ordinary Jews could not afford to drink wine unless it was a special occasion such as Passover.
d. In Matthew Jesus says that the betrayer is one who dips into the same dish. This could be the sauce Haroseth, a mixture of apples and spices which was eaten at the Passover. However, sauces were eaten at other meals.
e. A hymn was sung before they went out to the Mount of Olives. This would fit in with the singing of the Hallel (Psalms 114–118) at the end of the Passover meal.

Points against

a. Mark may have chosen to describe the Last Supper as a Passover meal to show that for Christians it had been replaced by the Eucharist.
b. The food usually eaten at the Passover meal, eg. roast lamb, bitter herbs etc. is not mentioned. The special words to commemorate the escape from Egypt are also not mentioned.

Prediction of the Betrayal
Matthew 26:20–25; Mark 14:17–21; Luke 22:17–19; John 13:21–30

Jesus predicted that one of the disciples would betray him. This would fulfil the prophecy in Psalm 41:9,
> 'Even my bosom friend in whom I trusted,
> who ate my bread, has lifted up his heel against me.'

Though Judas was acting in accordance with God's plan he could not escape judgement. 'It would have been better for that man never to have been born.'

The Eucharistic Words
Matthew 26:26–29; Mark 14:22–25; Luke 22:17–19; John has his version earlier in Jesus' ministry, 6:53–57

Jesus followed the usual pattern of a Jewish meal by blessing the bread, breaking it and passing it round. In this way the people at the meal shared in the blessing. The same happened with the wine at the end of the meal. Jesus was demonstrating that the disciples would share not only in the blessing but also in the results of his death.

    a. 'Take; this is my body.'

    b. 'This is my blood of the covenant which is poured out for many.'

Jesus was the sacrifice whose death would bring about the New Covenant prophesied by Jeremiah (31:31–34). Blood was used to seal a covenant. In Exodus 24:6–8 Moses threw half the blood of the sacrifice over the altar and half over the people. The New Covenant was to be sealed by the blood of Jesus.

Additional Information:

1. *Matthew*   26:28, adds that Jesus' blood was poured out for the forgiveness of sins. He is probably quoting from Isaiah 53:12.

2.   *Luke*   a. 22:24–28, also includes a dispute amongst the disciples about who was the most important. (Mark has this earlier, 9:34–35). Jesus' answer was that the greatest would become the least.

            b. 22:35–38, Jesus told them that they must now take a purse and buy a sword. This is in contrast to the mission of the seventy (10:1–12). This suggests that Jesus expected that the persecution and suffering which leads up to the final Judgement would begin with his death. The disciples must prepare themselves. Jesus identified himself with the suffering servant by quoting from Isaiah 53:12.

            c. 22:29–34, Luke describes Jesus' prediction of Peter's denial as taking place during the Last Supper. (see below)

3.   *John*   a. 13:3–11, Before the meal Jesus took a towel and washed the feet of his disciples. This was usually done by a servant. Jesus was demonstrating his love for them and acting out his teaching that the greatest must be the least. The master is not greater than the servant.

            b. Chapters 14–17 contain teaching, some of which is discussed in the chapter on John's Gospel.

            c. 13:36–38, John also records the prediction of Peter's denial as taking place during the Last Supper. (see below)

11. The prediction of Peter's denial
Matthew 26:30–35; Mark 14:26–31; Luke 22:31–34; John 13:36–38

This takes place at the Mount of Olives in Matthew and Mark. Pilgrims were not allowed to leave Jerusalem during the Passover but the Mount of Olives was within the boundary of Jerusalem. Quoting from Zechariah 13:7 Jesus explained that after he was taken the disciples would scatter but after he was raised he could go to Galilee. Peter said he would never abandon Jesus but Jesus replied that before the cock crowed (twice in Mark) he would deny him three times. The keeping of cocks in Jerusalem may not have been allowed at the time. The phrase might just have meant 'in the early morning' or 'cock crow' might have been the bugle call for the changing of the Roman guard at the Antonia fortress.

12. The garden of Gethsemane
Matthew 26:36–56; Mark 14:32–51; Luke 22:39–53; John 18:1–11

'Gethsemane' probably meant 'olive press'. Jesus took Peter, James and John further into the garden with him whilst he prayed, and told them to watch and pray. In Mark, Jesus goes to pray three times and returns each time to find the disciples asleep. In Luke there is only one prayer. John does not describe one at all.

Jesus' Prayer: Abba, Father, all things are possible to thee, remove this cup from me; yet not what I will but what thou wilt.

Mark 14:36

'Abba' was a children's word for father used in every day language. There is no parallel in Jewish prayers for addressing God as 'Abba' and it expresses the unique relationship between Jesus and God. In this prayer Jesus is asking that the 'cup' (suffering) could be taken away from him. This could be a plea for God to bring in his Kingdom without suffering being necessary. The instruction to the disciples to watch and pray would then mean that they had to prepare themselves for the imminent coming of the Kingdom. According to the story no-one overheard this prayer but in view of its content it is unlikely to have been completely invented.

Because the four Gospels are in close agreement it is possible that the earliest traditions of the death of Jesus began with the arrest. Judas kissed Jesus as a sign of whom to arrest. A kiss was a common form of greeting between rabbis and disciples, but the Greek word used for 'kiss' here is of a more affectionate kind. This makes Judas' betrayal even worse. The crowd had been sent by the chief priests to arrest Jesus. John records that Roman soldiers arrested him. A disciple (named as Peter in John) cut off the ear of the High Priest's servant (named as Malchus in John) and Luke says that Jesus healed it.

Mark records the incident of a boy escaping after his sheet had been caught. 'Naked' means 'only in a tunic'. Tradition says that this was John Mark (the author of the Gospel) but it is strange that he left such an enigmatic verse and did not include more details.

13. The trial before the Sanhedrin
Matthew 26:57, 59–68; Mark 14:53–65; Luke 22:54, 66–70. John 18:12–14, 19–24

The Sanhedrin was the official Jewish court of justice. It had seventy one members, with the High Priest (Caiaphas) as President. The trial of Jesus before the Sanhedrin does not agree with information about procedure found in Jewish literature. However, this information comes from after A.D. 70 when the Temple had been destroyed and the Jews expelled from Jerusalem, so that the procedure may have been different at the time of Jesus.

    a. The court was not usually held in the High Priest's house.

    b. Trials which could result in execution could not take place during the night and had to be held on two consecutive days. (Matthew and Mark have the trial as taking place during the night.)

    c. Witnesses were warned that they would be punished by death for giving false evidence.

    d. Witnesses were examined separately and two witnesses had to agree.

    e. Witnesses for the defence were usually called.

Luke records the trial as taking place during the day. John has preliminary questioning by Annas (Caiaphas' father-in-law) followed by the trial before the Sanhedrin.

Jesus is recorded as admitting openly that he was the Messiah but he was not technically guilty of blasphemy. The High Priest tore his robe, a formal act when blasphemy was declared. Blasphemy was punishable by death by stoning according to the Jewish law. It has been suggested that at the time of Jesus the Jews were not allowed to use the death penalty. The Gospels seem intent on putting the blame on the Jews and not the Romans.

One way of resolving the difficulties raised by the trial is to say that it was not a proper trial but was merely a hearing to collect evidence to put before Pilate.

Jesus is blindfolded, spat upon and hit and told to say who hit him.

14. Peter's denial
Matthew 26:69–75; Mark 14:66–72; Luke 22:56–62; John 18:16–18

There are minor variations in the different Gospel accounts, eg. who the accusers were varies slightly. However the essential details of the story are the same: Peter was accused three times of having been with Jesus and each time he denied it. He had probably been seen with Jesus as he taught in Jerusalem and his Galilean dialect confirmed the suspicion. This story is thought to have come from Peter himself.

15. The trial before Pilate
Matthew 27:11–26; Mark 15:1–15; Luke 23:2–3, 18–25; John 18:29–19:16

Pilate was the Procurator of Judaea from 25–36 A.D. He usually lived in Caesarea but at Passover time moved to Jerusalem to maintain order. He was a merciless and obstinate man who was well known for his cruelty. The picture of Pilate presented by the Gospels is very different from historical accounts. It was in the interests of the Gospel writers, who had to exist in a Roman world to show Roman justice as very sympathetic and Pilate as being a fair and moderate judge. The Gospel writers wanted to stress that the Jews, not the Romans, were responsible for the death of Jesus. They describe Pilate as being unwilling to condemn Jesus, and attempting to get round it by:

a. sending Jesus to Herod. (This is only in Luke's Gospel.)
b. offering to set Jesus free instead of Barabbas.
c. washing his hands to demonstrate that he was not responsible. (Only in Matthew.)

The charges brought against Jesus had to be altered since blasphemy was not a crime under Roman law. Jesus was charged with:

a. Claiming to the the King of the Jews.
b. Inciting the people not to pay taxes to Caesar. (Only in Luke.)
c. Claiming to be the Messiah. (Only in Luke.)

If Jesus had been claiming to be the King of the Jews this would have been a threat against Roman rule. According to the Synoptic Gospels Jesus made no reply to the charges except to answer Pilate's question, 'Are you the King of the Jews?' by saying, 'You have said so', thus leaving the question open. Pilate must answer the question for himself, as must the reader of the Gospel.

There is no historical evidence for the custom of releasing a prisoner at Passover, although it was not unknown for the governor to grant an amnesty in a particular case. Barabbas was a nationalist who was popular with the crowd. It is very unlikely that a man of Pilate's character would consult the crowd in the way described in the Gospels. The choice is described as being between freedom for Barabbas or death for Jesus but Jesus had not been found guilty at this point. It is possible that some manuscripts of Matthew which record Barabbas as being called 'Jesus Barabbas' are in fact correct. The early church would not have wanted the name 'Jesus' to be associated with Barabbas and that is why it was dropped from later manuscripts. There may have been a tradition that the people of Jerusalem had petitioned Pilate for the release of Jesus Barabbas. The Gospel writers used this tradition to show that the people saved Jesus Barabbas, the criminal, but allowed Jesus the Messiah to be crucified.

Additional Information:

1. *Matthew* a. Pilate's wife had a dream warning Pilate to have nothing to do with Jesus (27:19). Dreams play an important part in Matthew's Gospel.

               b. Pilate washed his hands in public to demonstrate that he was not responsible for the death of Jesus (27:24–25). It is very unlikely that he did this but it emphasises the responsibility of the Jews for the death of Jesus.

2.   *Luke*   When Pilate realised that Jesus was from Galilee he sent Jesus to Herod Antipas who happened to be in Jerusalem at the time. Herod ruled Galilee. According to Luke, Herod was pleased to see Jesus and wanted to see him perform a miracle but Jesus remained silent. Herod sent him back to Pilate in a purple robe. It is possible that Luke may have been thinking about Psalm 2:1–2 when he included this incident: 'the rulers take counsel together, against the Lord and his anointed.' (23:6–12)

3.   *John* a. Pilate told the Jewish leaders to deal with Jesus them-

selves but they protested that they could not carry out the death sentence. (18:31)

b. Pilate and Jesus had a discussion about kingship and truth. Jesus admitted to Pilate that he was a king but his kingdom was not of this world because if it was his disciples would fight to save him. Pilate asked 'What is truth?' but did not wait for an answer. (18:36–38)

c. Once again Pilate told the Jewish leaders to deal with Jesus themselves because he could not find him guilty. Jesus said that Pilate would have no power over him unless it had been given to him by God. The Jews threatened Pilate by saying that if he allowed Jesus to go he would be no friend of Caesar. Reluctantly Pilate handed Jesus over to be crucified. (19:6–12)

The Gospel accounts of the trials of Jesus emphasise three points:

a. The Roman authorities were not responsible for the death of Jesus. If Pilate condemned Jesus as a rebel then this could have been used as evidence that Christians were a threat to Roman power.

b. The Jews were responsible for the death of Jesus because they failed to recognise that he was the Messiah.

c. Jesus did not attempt to defend himself but gave himself up to God's plan.

If the Gospel accounts are taken literally then Pilate had difficulty in deciding to condemn Jesus. This could have been for various reasons.

a. He may have believed that Jesus was innocent. Roman justice had a high reputation. Condemning an innocent man would damage this reputation.

b. He may have not wanted to give in to the Jews on what was merely a religious question.

c. He may have been afraid of trouble breaking out at the Passover when Jerusalem was crowded with pilgrims. This might have resulted in him being recalled to Rome.

d. Some people have argued that Pilate might have believed that Jesus was 'a god' since the Romans believed in many gods.

16. The Scourging
Matthew 27:27–31; Mark 15:16–20; Luke 23:11; John 19:2–3

Scourging usually took place before crucifixion. (John however has the scourging in the middle of the trial before Pilate.) The prisoner was tied to a pillar and beaten with leather whips which had pieces of metal at the end. They mocked Jesus as a king by putting a purple robe on him and a crown of thorns.

17. The Crucifixion
Matthew 27:32–55; Mark 15:21–40; Luke 23:26–49; John 19:17–37

There are differences in the Gospel accounts of the death of Jesus. It is impossible to piece them together to form one account. They each express clearly the mystery of Jesus' death. The most important differences will be noted under each Gospel.

Criminals condemned to crucifixion had to carry the cross-beam of their cross. (The upright was already in position.) According to the Synoptics, Simon of Cyrene was forced to carry the beam for Jesus. Mark describes Simon as 'the father of Alexander and Rufus' who were members of the Church. John does not mention this incident. This may be because some people (Gnostics) claimed that Simon had changed places with Jesus and had been crucified instead of him.

The crucifixion took place on a hill called Golgotha. It was usual to crucify people where they would be seen by others as a warning. The condemned man was stripped and his wrists nailed to the cross beam before it was hoisted up and fixed to the upright. The feet were tied with leather strips or were nailed. A block of wood half way up the cross supported the body. Crucifixion was a very slow and painful death. A tablet, inscribed with the name of the criminal, his home town and his crime, was fixed to the cross. Pilate wrote, 'Jesus of Nazareth, King of the Jews.' John adds that the Jewish leaders wanted Pilate to alter it to 'he claimed to be King of the Jews' but Pilate refused. John also adds that the inscription was in three languages, Hebrew, Latin and Greek. It was the custom for the Roman auxiliary guards to divide the criminal's clothes amongst themselves. This is seen as the fulfilment of Psalm 22:18. It was also customary for some women to offer the criminals a drink of spiced wine to reduce their suffering. (Proverbs 31:6–7 said that they should give wine to those in bitter distress.) Jesus refused this drink.

Jesus was mocked by those standing around the cross. Mark records them as tempting Jesus to come down from the cross so that they would believe.

All the Gospels record that at the sixth hour there was darkness until the ninth hour. Attempts have been made to explain the darkness:

a. It could be a fulfilment of Old Testament passages such as Amos 8:9,

> 'I will make the sun go down at noon,
> and darken the earth in broad daylight.'

b. It could have been an eclipse. This is unlikely at a full moon.

c. Similar events were recorded at the deaths of great rabbis or leaders, eg. Julius Caesar.

Matthew and Mark say that Jesus cried out, in Aramaic, 'My God, my God, why hast thou forsaken me?' This is from Psalm 22:1. This could be interpreted as a cry of despair but the Psalm taken as a whole is a triumphant one. The opening of the Psalm was used as a prayer in time of trouble.

The crowd is described as misunderstanding the cry as a plea to Elijah. Jesus was offered vinegar (a mixture of vinegar, water and eggs which the Romans drank.) It is not clear who offered him the sponge or whether the motive was one of pity or mockery. According to Matthew and Mark, Jesus uttered a loud cry and died. It would have been very unusual for anyone near to death on the cross to have the strength to cry out. This was perhaps what impressed the centurion who in Mark's Gospel declared that 'this man was the Son of God.' The Synoptic Gospels record that at Jesus' death the curtain of the Temple was torn in two from top to bottom. There were in fact two curtains in the Temple, one separating the Holy Place and one the Holy of Holies (see the diagram of the Temple on pg 18). It is likely that the one in the Holy of Holies is meant. The high priest entered this part only once a year, on the Day of Atonement. The tearing of the curtain symbolised that the old order had been replaced and access to God had been given to everyone.

Additional Information:

Matthew   Matthew mentions that there was an earthquake at Jesus' death and the tombs opened and the bodies of the saints were raised. Earthquakes appear in legends about great events eg. the death of Caesar. It is likely that the reference to the dead being raised should really come after the earthquake mentioned by Matthew at the resurrection, since it does not fit in with the idea that Jesus was the first to be raised (1 Corinthians 15:20).

Luke   Luke records the first words of Jesus on the cross as being, 'Father, forgive them; for they know not what they do.' He also includes a conversation between Jesus and the two thieves crucified with him. One of the thieves mocked Jesus but the other recognised that Jesus was innocent. Jesus told him that he would he with him in Paradise. According to Luke Jesus cried out aloud. 'Father, into Thy hands I commit my spirit,' (Psalm 31) before he died.

John   John includes an account of Jesus telling his mother and 'the disciple Jesus loved' (John) that in future they were to be as mother and son. Jesus died with the words, 'It is finished'.

A Summary of Jesus's words on the Cross

1. 'Father, forgive them; for they know not what they do.' (Lk 23:34)
2. 'Truly, I say to you, today you will be with me in Paradise.' (Lk 23:43)
3. 'My God, my God, why hast thou forsaken me?' Mt 27:46, (Mk 15:34)
4. 'Woman, behold your son!', 'Behold, your mother!' (Jhn 19:26–27)
5. 'I thirst.' Jhn 19:28
6. 'It is finished.' Jhn 19:30
7. 'Father, into thy hands I commit my spirit.' (Lk 23:46)

18. The Burial
Matthew 27:57–61; Mark 15:42–47; Luke 23:50–56; John 19:38–42

The burial of Jesus was important because it showed that Jesus was really dead. Some of those who saw the body laid in the tomb also saw the empty tomb. Mark says that it was 6 pm; but if so it would already have been the Sabbath and they would not have been allowed to bury the body. It is possible that Mark meant 4 pm. It was the Jewish custom that a body should be buried on the day of death. They buried the dead outside the city in tombs cut out of the rocks, or caves. The body was laid on a shelf and a circular stone was placed in front of the tomb.

Joseph of Arimathaea was described as a respected member of the council, this could mean the Sanhedrin.

John adds that the criminals crucified with Jesus had their legs broken but since Jesus was already dead he had a spear thrust into his side. The wound flowed with blood and water. John sees this as fulfilment of Psalm 34:20 'He keeps all his bones; not one of them is broken.'

Blood and water, have symbolic significance in John's Gospel. (See the Chapter on John's Gospel). John states that Nicodemus anointed the body of Jesus.

Matthew adds that the Jews asked for a Roman guard to be put on the tomb so that Jesus' disciples could not steal the body and claim that he had risen.

Work Section

Section A

1. Why did Jesus deserve death under Jewish Law?
2. Why might the predictions about Jesus' death have been made up by the Gospel writers?
3. How did the disciples respond to Jesus' predictions?
4. What instructions did Jesus give to the disciples when he sent them to fetch the colt?
5. What did the people do when they saw Jesus riding into Jerusalem?
6. How did the chief priests and scribes react to the cleansing of the Temple?
7. Why were some people indignant when the woman anointed Jesus' head?
8. What extra information does John's Gospel give about this incident?
9. What instructions did Jesus give to the disciples who were sent to prepare for the Passover meal?
10. How does Luke describe Jesus' anguish in the Garden of Gethsemane?
11. What did Jesus say to the crowd who had come to arrest him in the Garden of Gethsemane?
12. What did the false witnesses accuse Jesus of saying?
13. What did Jesus reply when the High Priest asked him, 'Are you the Christ, the Son of the Blessed?'
14. What was the name of the High Priest?
15. What was Jesus found guilty of by the Sanhedrin?
16. Where was Peter when he denied Jesus for the first time?
17. What did Peter say after he had been accused of being a disciple of Jesus for the third time?
18. What happened after the cock crowed a second time?
19. Who was Pilate?
20. What was Jesus charged with before Pilate?
21. What choice did Pilate give to the crowd?

22. What extra information does Matthew give about the trial before Pilate?
23. Describe the conversation between Jesus and Pilate recorded in John's Gospel.
24. How did the soldiers mock Jesus?
25. Who was compelled to carry Jesus' cross?
26. What does 'Golgotha' mean?
27. What happened to Jesus' clothes?
28. Why were the Jewish leaders annoyed about the inscription on the cross?
29. How was Jesus tempted on the cross?
30. What unnatural events occurred during the crucifixion?
31. Who witnessed Jesus' death?
32. Who asked Pilate for Jesus' body?
33. Who anointed the body of Jesus according to John's Gospel?
34. According to Matthew's Gospel, what happened the day after the crucifixion?

Section B

35. How did Jesus prepare his disciples for his coming death? What signs are there they they did not understand what he was saying? 10,10

36. Describe the entry of Jesus into Jerusalem. Why did Jesus choose to enter in this way? 12,8

37. Give an account of the cleansing of the Temple. Describe how the Jewish leaders plotted to arrest Jesus. 12,8

38. Describe the parts played in the accounts of Jesus' death by, **a** Peter, **b** Judas, **c** Joseph of Arimathaea, and **d** Nicodemus. 8,6,4,2

39. Relate the story of the anointing of Jesus at Bethany. What is the significance of this event? 12,8

40. Describe the Last Supper according to the Synoptic Gospels. What are the arguments for and against it being a Passover meal? 12,8

41. Give an account of the Last Supper according to John's Gospel. What teaching does Jesus give about the true vine? 12,8

42. 'Even though they all fall away, I will not.' Why did Peter say these words and how did he later break his promise? 6,14

43. Describe the events which took place in the garden of Gethsemane. 20

44. Give an account of Jesus' trial in front of **a** the Sanhedrin and **b** Pilate. 8,12

45. What part was played by Pilate in the trials of Jesus? Why did he have difficulty in condemning Jesus? 12,8

46. Describe the parts played by **a** Caiaphas, **b** Herod, and **c** Pilate, in condemning Jesus. 8,4,8

47. How do the Gospel accounts stress that the Jews and not the Romans were responsible for the death of Jesus? 20

48. Describe the crucifixion of Jesus. List the words spoken by Jesus whilst he was on the cross. 13,7

49. What was the response of the people who witnessed the Crucifixion? What happened to Jesus' body after his death? 12,8

Section C

50. What are the similarities and differences between the death of Jesus and people such as Gandhi and Martin Luther King?

51. If Jesus had not been crucified would Christianity have been founded?

52. Why is Easter more important than Christmas?

The Resurrection

The Gospel stories of the trial and death of Jesus contain many similarities. However, the Resurrection stories are very different. It is impossible to work out what actually happened although various explanations have been given. It is important to begin by looking at the four different accounts. These have been summarised in the chart on pages 158–160. It is necessary to read through the four accounts in the Bible, consulting the chart at the same time. Incidents marked with asterisks will be discussed in further detail.

1. Mark

Mark has the shortest account of the resurrection. The Gospel ends at 16:8 with the story of the women running away, too frightened to tell anyone what had happened. 16:9–20 is a later addition which was composed by gathering incidents from the other Gospels.

Why does Mark end here?

It is a very strange ending for a book which is supposed to be about 'good news'. It leaves Peter who is the leader of the early Church as the one who denied Jesus. Various theories have been put forward to explain this:

a. Mark intended to write more but was prevented from doing so by illness or arrest. However, it is rather a coincidence that he broke off at a point which might be a possible ending. The addition of even one more Greek word would have shown that it was unfinished.

b. Mark did write more but the manuscript was lost. It was common for the last pages of manuscripts to be lost or damaged as a result of frequent copying but if it was lost then it could have been copied from a complete manuscript. If it had been lost before any copies had been made then it would seem likely that Mark would have rewritten it.

Matthew	Mark	Luke	John
On the first day of the week Mary Magdalene, and the other Mary went to look at the grave. (28:1)	After the Sabbath Mary Magdalene, Mary the mother of James and Salome, went to the tomb to anoint the body. (16:1–2)	After the Sabbath the women (Mary Magdalene, Joanna and Mary the mother of James and the other women, went to anoint the body. (24:1,10)	On the first day of the week Mary Magdalene went to the tomb. (20:1)
After a great earthquake an angel rolled away the stone and sat on it. The guards lay as dead. (28:2–4)	The women wondered who would roll away the stone but it was already rolled back when they arrived. (16:3–4)	The stone had already been rolled away and the tomb was empty. (24:3)	The stone had already been rolled away. (20:16)
The angel was dressed in clothes as white as snow. He told the women not to be afraid. Jesus had risen. They must tell the disciples to meet him in Galilee. 28:5–7)	A young man in white inside the tomb told the women that Jesus had risen. They must tell the disciples and Peter to meet Jesus in Galilee as he told them. (16:5–7)	Two men in dazzling clothes asked why they looked for the living amongst the dead. They must remember how Jesus had said that he would rise. (24:4–7)	
The women left quickly with fear and great joy and ran to tell the disciples. (28:8)	They fled from the tomb trembling with astonishment. They were afraid so they said nothing to anyone. (16:8)	They returned from the tomb and told the eleven and others but the apostles did not believe them. (24:8–11)	Mary ran to tell Peter and John. (20:2)

Matthew	Mark	Luke	John
As they left Jesus met them. They worshipped him and Jesus told them to tell the disciples to meet him in Galilee. (28:9–10)			Peter and John ran to the tomb and seeing the folded grave-clothes they believed that he had risen. They returned home. (20:3–10)*
The guard told the chief priests what had happened. They bribed the soldiers to say that Jesus' body had been stolen by the disciples whilst they were asleep, and they would see that they did not get into trouble.			Mary remained weeping. Two angels in white inside the tomb asked why she was weeping. She said it was because they had taken Jesus' body away. Jesus appeared but at first she thought he was the gardener. She told the disciples. (20:11–18)*

Matthew	Mark	Luke	John
		Jesus appeared to two disciples as they walked to Emmaus. (24:13–32)**	Jesus appeared in the Upper Room once when Thomas was not there and once when he was. (20:191–29)**
		Whilst they were in the Upper Room telling the disciples what had happened, Jesus appeared. He ate fish to prove that he was not a ghost. He explained why he had to suffer and told them to stay in Jerusalem to await the gift of the Holy Spirit. (24:33–49)**	
The eleven go to Galilee. They saw Jesus and worshipped him although some doubted. Jesus told them to make disciples of all nations and baptise. He promised to be with them always. (28:16–20)		Jesus takes them out to Bethany where he blesses them and then leaves them. (24:50–51)	Jesus did many other signs which are not recorded. (20:30–31) Jesus appeared in Galilee whilst the disciples were fishing. There was a miraculous catch of fish. Peter promised to care for Jesus' sheep. (21:1–25;

Many scholars now think that 16:8 is where Mark intended to finish. The Gospel shows that Jesus has risen and portrays the astonishment of the women. Mark's readers would know that Jesus' resurrection had been revealed to other people. It can be seen as a very subtle ending!

2. Matthew

Matthew uses Mark as its basis but there are some important differences:
  a. The women go to look at the tomb, not to anoint the body. Matthew would probably know that in Palestine it would have been impossible for a body to be anointed on the third day since it would have already started to decompose.
  b. They see the stone rolled away during an earthquake. This could be to stress the miraculous.
  c. Jesus appears to the women as they leave the tomb.
  d. The guards are bribed by the chief priests to say that the disciples stole the body whilst they were asleep, (although their story would be implausible since they could not have known what happened if they had been asleep!). Matthew adds that the Jews believed this story. He may therefore have included the story about the guards as a defence against this accusation.

3. Luke

Luke used Mark's acount and although he did not know Matthew's Gospel he may have known some of the same traditions. The women at the tomb are the same women who had followed Jesus from Galilee.

a) The road to Emmaus
24:13–32

Two disciples (only Cleopas is named) meet Jesus on the road to Emmaus which is seven miles from Jerusalem. They do not recognise him. They explain that Jesus of Nazareth, whom they hoped would have redeemed Israel, has been crucified. Some women have said that the tomb is empty and an angel had said that Jesus was alive. Some of the disciples had also seen the empty tomb. Using the scriptures Jesus teaches them that the Messiah had to suffer before being glorified. When they reach

Emmaus they invite Jesus to stay. When he blesses and breaks the bread they recognise him. Immediately he vanishes and they rush back to Jerusalem to tell the disciples. However they discover that Jesus has already appeared to Peter, and the disciples now believe.

This story is only in Luke. Peter is shown to be the first person to see the risen Jesus. This agrees with Paul's list of resurrection appearances in 1 Corinthians 15:3. However some scholars have suggested that this verse (24:34) is a later addition to stress the importance of Peter. The fact that they recognised Jesus in the act of breaking bread suggests a link with the Eucharist. Christians can 'witness' Jesus at the breaking of bread and find faith.

b) The upper Room
24:33–49

Whilst they are talking Jesus appears. They are afraid because they think that he is a ghost. (This is strange since Luke says that they now believe that Jesus has risen.) Jesus shows them his hands and feet and tells them to touch him to prove that he is not a spirit. Some of the disciples are overjoyed but others still doubt. Jesus eats some fish as further proof of his physical resurrection. After teaching them about the necessity for the Messiah to suffer, Jesus commands them to preach and to wait in Jerusalem for the gift of the Holy Spirit.

4. John

a The race to the tomb
20:1–10

Mary Magdalene goes alone to visit the tomb and not to anoint the body since Nicodemus did this before the burial. She sees that the stone has been rolled away from the tomb and runs to tell Peter and John that the body has been stolen. Some scholars think that the story of the race to the tomb was inserted into the account of Mary's visit. 'The disciple Jesus loved', that is John, reaches the tomb first but Peter enters first and after seeing the folded grave clothes they believe.

b The appearance to Mary
20:11–18

After Peter and John have left, Mary stands outside the tomb weeping. When she looks in she sees two angels who ask her why she is weeping. She replies that the body of her Lord has been taken away. Mary then turns and sees Jesus but she does not recognise him. Jesus also asks her why she is weeping and who she is looking for. Thinking that he is the gardener, she asks him where the body is. Jesus says 'Mary' and she recognises him and calls him Rabbi. Jesus tells her not to touch him because he has not yet ascended but to go and tell the disciples. This is a strange request since it suggests that Jesus is a ghost, whereas in the story of Thomas, Jesus proves that he is not. The best explanation is that the verse means that although she could touch him he wanted her instead to go to tell the disciples that he had risen.

c The appearance in the upper room
20:19–29

Jesus enters the locked room where the disciples are together. After showing them his hands and side Jesus breathes the Holy Spirit onto them. Thomas was not present and he refuses to believe unless he can touch the nail-prints and put his hand into Jesus' side. A week later Jesus reappears and tells Thomas to touch him. Thomas believes. Jesus says that it is better to believe without seeing. John is probably stressing that in future people will have to believe without tangible proof.

    N.B. John's Gospel originally ended at 20:31. Chapter 21 is an addition. Most scholars are agreed that it is by a different author. The appearance which it records would make more sense if it was a first appearance.

d The Sea of Galilee
Chapter 21

Peter and some of the other disciples have been fishing unsuccessfully on the Sea of Galilee during the night. Jesus appears on the shore. They do not recognise him. He tells them to let the net over the right side of the boat. They do so and catch so many fish that they are unable to haul the net in but have to drag it ashore. 'The disciple Jesus loved' realises that it is Jesus. Peter immediately jumps into the water (having put on his coat to make himself decent) and swims to Jesus. They have caught one hundred and fifty three fish. This number may represent all the followers of Jesus.

Afterwards Jesus asks Peter three times if he loves him, and each time Peter replies that he does. Jesus commands him to feed his sheep. (This might be to cancel out the three denials.)

N.B. Luke records a similar miracle in the call of the first disciples, Lk 5:1–11.

The resurrection stories contain difficulties which cannot be resolved. The tomb is empty, Jesus can be touched and he eats in front of his disciples. However he is not easily recognisable. Some of the disciples who see the risen Jesus have doubts. It is impossible to say what actually happened. All the Gospels portray the mysterious and overwhelming nature of the resurrection.

An alternative to the traditional understanding of a bodily resurrection, is that Jesus 'came to life' in the sense that the disciples understood what he had said. They went out to preach about Jesus instead of hiding away afraid of the Jews. In this way Jesus came to life again.

Work Section

Section A

1. List the similarities between the four accounts.
2. In Matthew, what happened when the women were leaving the tomb?
3. Describe what happened when the guards told the chief priests what had happened.
4. What happened when the eleven disciples met Jesus in Galilee, according to Matthew's account?
5. Who were the two disciples who were travelling to Emmaus?
6. What did the disciples tell the stranger about what had happened in Jerusalem?
7. What did the stranger explain to them?
8. How did they recognise that their companion was Jesus?
9. What had happened by the time that they returned to Jerusalem?
10. According to Luke's Gospel, how did Jesus prove that he was not a ghost?
11. What did Jesus explain to the disciples in the upper room, according to Luke's Gospel?
12. How does Luke's Gospel end?
13. What happened when Peter and John ran to the tomb?
14. What did Mary ask 'the gardener'?
15. Give an explanation of why Jesus told Mary not to touch him.
16. What did Jesus say to the disciples in the upper room on his first visit, according to John's Gospel?
17. What happened when Peter realised that Jesus was on the beach, according to John 21?
18. Describe the conversation which took place between Jesus and Peter after breakfast.

Section B

19. According to the Gospels, what events took place at the tomb where Jesus was buried? 20

20. Describe the part played by **a** Mary Magdalene, **b** 'the disciple Jesus loved', and **c** Thomas, in the resurrection appearances. 8,4,8

21. Describe the visit of the women to the tomb according to Mark's Gospel. Account for the strange ending of Mark's Gospel. 12,8

22. Give an account of the story of the road to Emmaus, and the appearance in the upper room, according to Luke's Gospel. 10,10

23. Describe the visit of Peter and John to the tomb, and the meeting with Jesus in Galilee, according to John's Gospel. 6,14

24. What evidence is there in the Gospels that the disciples were slow to believe in the resurrection? 20

Section C

25. How and why do the resurrection stories stress the importance of Peter?

26. Read 1 Corinthians 15:3–9 and list the appearances mentioned by Paul. Underline those which are also found in the Gospels.

27. Why do you think that the extra verses were added to Mark's Gospel?

28. Explain the change in attitude of the disciples between the arrest of Jesus (Mk 14:32–72) and the Day of Pentecost, (Acts 2:14–41)

29. Do the Gospels really supply evidence for the Resurrection?

30. Would the resurrection make sense if Jesus did not rise bodily?

31. If the Turin Shroud was found to have been made in the first century, would it prove the resurrection? Should Christians need physical evidence of the resurrection?

32. Suggestions for further reading:
The Turin Shroud,
The Resurrection of Jesus of Nazareth, Willi Marxsen
Who Moved the Stone? William Morrison

The Gospel of John

1. Author and date

The traditional author of the Gospel, the three Epistles and the Revelation is John the Disciple. The legend of his life is that he was arrested in Ephesus for being a Christian, he was sent as a slave to the mines in Patmos and he died there when nearly a hundred years old. There is little evidence for this account of his life and none to support the belief that John the disciple was the author of the Gospel. It is most unlikely that the author of the Gospel also wrote any of the Epistles since the style and ideas are so different. The main argument against John the disciple being the author of the Gospel is that it is very difficult to believe that a Galilean fisherman could have written such a work. It is thought to have been the last of the four Gospels to be written. It is such a unique book that scholars rarely agree about its origins, purpose and date.

Of the many theories, the one which has most support, is that the Gospel of John was written at Ephesus in about 110 A.D. This was an important port in Eastern Turkey. Some of the stories and ideas may have been preserved by John the Disciple and passed on to the author of the Gospel by his followers. It was therefore not written by the disciple but carried his authority. Some scholars think that because the enemies of Jesus are presented as the 'Jews' then the Gospel was written for Christians who belonged to Jewish communities outside Palestine. Another view is that the Gospel was written for Gentiles since it borrows ideas from Greek philosophy. It was once thought that geographical details given in the Gospel were inventions of the author, but modern archaeology is showing that he gives a good account of Southern Palestine.

2. Themes

The main belief is that eternal life is not a future event but begins immediately with faith in Jesus. Those who accept that Jesus is the Son of God and try to follow his teaching are saved. The disciples who witnessed the 'works' that Jesus did become united with him and with God. In the same way, those who believe in Jesus after listening to the disciples are also united with Jesus and God. The proof that the Gospel is true was the work of Jesus (miracles and teaching) and the faith of people in Jesus.

The Gospel is very different from the Synoptic Gospels. It does not have the form of a life history. It consists mostly of conversations and speeches in which Jesus explains his ideas to people who cannot understand the real meaning of what he says. When he speaks to those who have been chosen to believe then he openly claims to be the Messiah. It is most unlikely that the Gospel contains the actual words of Jesus. This style of writing was found in Greek philosophy. The author put into the mouths of speakers the sort of things that they would have said, not the actual speeches that the historical person had used. The author of John's Gospel is presenting his own understanding of Jesus in such a way as to help other people realize that Jesus was and is the 'way, and the truth, and the life' of God.

The Gospel uses many symbols or images to explain the importance of Jesus. These are taken from Jewish mysticism and Greek philosophy to help the reader understand. However, today, these symbols themselves have to be explained before they can be understood since we do not think in the same way as the people for whom the Gospel was written. Some of these symbols are Word, Father, Son, Way, Truth, Life, Light and Bread. The Fourth Gospel is therefore the most difficult of the Gospels to understand, but because of this, it is also the most profound and the greatest.

3. Nicodemus
John 3:1–21; 7:50, 51; 19:38–52

He is mentioned on three occasions in John's Gospel but not in the Synoptics. He was a Pharisee who became a secret follower of Jesus.

John 3:1–21 He went to talk with Jesus during the night. He believed that Jesus was from God because of what Jesus did, but he could not fully understand the teaching. He asked a series of questions which allowed Jesus to explain how a person can be born into the Kingdom. The conversation is artificial but may contain genuine sayings of Jesus which are expanded in the Gospel. The Christian is reborn in baptism. Nicodemus was confused by the image of birth which he accepted literally as a physical, not a spiritual event. The new birth is achieved by faith in Jesus as the Son of God. The choice is between the darkness of evil and the light of God which reveals the truth.

John 7:50, 51 When the chief priests and Pharisees wanted to arrest Jesus during the Feast of the Tabernacles, Nicodemus defended his right to be heard before being judged. This suggests that Nicodemus belonged to the Sanhedrin.

John 19:38–42 Nicodemus helped Joseph of Arimathaea to bury Jesus. He brought an extraordinarily heavy amount of ointment for the corpse. It was a fitting quantity with which to bury the King of the Jews.

4. The woman by Jacob's Well
John 4:1–42

Jesus was travelling from Judea to Galilee along the mountain road through Samaria. There is a very deep well which was used between 1000 B.C. and 500 A.D. near the ruined city of Sichem. There is no explanation why the woman should have come out of her village to fetch water when there would have been a spring in the village. Like Nicodemus, she asked Jesus a series of naive questions which allowed him to explain the importance of living water. This was a symbol of the Spirit which would give the woman new life and energy. She cannot understand what he means until he tells her that she has had five husbands and is not married to the man with whom she lives. She then realised that he is a prophet. Jesus went on to tell her that a time would come when Samaritans will not worship God at their Temple in Samaria, nor Jews worship in Jerusalem, but all will worship God in spirit and truth. The woman claimed that the Messiah would reveal all things and Jesus told her that he was the Messiah.

When the disciples returned they were very surprised to find Jesus talking with the woman. A strict Jew would have thought her to be unclean. The woman went back to her city to tell people about Jesus. They invited him to stay. (This contrasts with the story of the Samaritan villagers who rejected Jesus and whom the disciples wanted to punish with fire from Heaven in Luke 9:51) Many of the people believed that Jesus was Saviour of the World. The story is combined with some teaching about the harvest. The disciples are reaping what others have sown as people believe in their preaching about Jesus.

5. The authority of Jesus
John 5:19–47; 7:1–52; 8:12–59

John 5:19–47 Sayings and short parables have been linked together into a long speech to the Jews explaining the authority of Jesus to act and speak. Jesus claims that the Father (God) has given him authority to act in God's name. The attitude of people to the Son (Jesus) is also their attitude to the Father. Jesus is claiming more than being a son of God as everyone is a son of God, or to be doing God's work as everyone can do God's work. He has a unique relationship. He is the Son who shares and inherits all of his Father's power. The Son will give judgement and Life. The evidence for this claim is:

1. John the Baptist identified Jesus as the Messiah.
2. The works which Jesus did.
3. Moses and the Scriptures point to Jesus.
4. The Father himself whose power enables Jesus to make the claim that he acts in God's name.

John 7:1–52 Jesus went to Jerusalem during the Feast of Tabernacles. This commemorated the time spent in the wilderness. People built shelters (tabernacles). As it was held during the Autumn it also became a celebration of the harvest. Jesus taught in the Temple and surprised the Jews by the power of what he said. He told them that it was not his own teaching, but God's. People wondered whether the authorities believed that Jesus was the Messiah since he was being allowed to teach when it was expected that he would be killed. However they knew where Jesus came from, whereas it was believed that no one would know where the Messiah came from. Another belief was that the Messiah would be descended from David and so come from Bethlehem. However, it was thought that Jesus came from Galilee. The Chief Priests and Pharisees sent men to arrest Jesus but they were so impressed by his teaching that they did not obey their orders.

John 8:12–59 The Jews cannot understand who Jesus is, or what he teaches, because they have rejected God. The contrast is brought out in several images, some of which are found in other passages of the Gospel.

1. Jesus is the Light of the World, but the Jews are in darkness.
2. Jesus brings God's judgement, but the Jews judge only by physical evidence (The Flesh).
3. Jesus is united in all he does with the Father (God), but the Jews do not know God.
4. Jesus is from above, but the Jews are from below (the world).

5. Jesus speaks and acts with God's authority, but the Jews will still kill him.
6. Those who believe in Jesus will become free, but those who do not will remain slaves to Sin.
7 God is the Father of Jesus, but not of the Jews who reject Jesus. Their father is the devil.
8. Jesus speaks the truth, but the Jews only believe lies.

The argument reaches a climax when Jesus claims to have existed before Abraham, the first Jew. They call Jesus a Samaritan and claim that he is possessed by a demon. This ends in an attempt to stone Jesus but he escapes.

This discussion seems unlikely to have taken place in the Temple during Jesus' life. It is the kind of angry debate which happened between Jews and Christians in the years after Jesus died. This hostility is found throughout the New Testament.

6. The Bread of Life
John 6:22–71

The Feeding of the Five Thousand and Walking on Water are followed in John's Gospel by teaching which uses the image of 'The Bread of Life'. Jesus warns the crowd which had followed him against being so impressed by the miracle of feeding that they fail to recognise its importance. Jesus is the real bread which God has sent to them. The ordinary bread is of no significance. All who believe in Jesus will be given eternal life. The Jews refuse to believe that Jesus is anything other than an ordinary man. Jesus extends the image further to tell them that only by eating his flesh will they have eternal life. This idea is totally repugnant to his enemies who understand it literally. Many of his own followers now desert him because they cannot 'stomach' his teaching. The twelve remain with Jesus because God has given them the ability to understand. This is the main theme of the whole Gospel. Those chosen by God will know that everything which Jesus says and does is the truth. Everyone else is repelled by Jesus because they have no understanding.

7. The woman taken in adultery
John 8:2–11

This story is not found in the oldest copies of the Gospel. It is therefore placed at the end of the Gospel or as a footnote since it does not belong at this point. It seems to be an authentic story which must have survived outside the Gospels until included in John's. The woman had been caught committing adultery and by Jewish law she ought to be punished by death (Deut. 22.22). The man should also be killed but he was not brought to Jesus. The usual punishment at this time would have been divorce without compensation. The Jews' demand that the woman be stoned was to test how Jesus applied the Law. The testimony of two witnesses was needed to prove an accusation, these witnesses then had the duty of beginning the execution (Deut. 17.6,7). In asking for anyone who had not sinned to give evidence Jesus was applying his own teaching from the Sermon on the Mount; that it was wrong to judge another when no one was perfect (Mt 7:1–5). Jewish Law relied upon the witnesses being completely trustworthy since their evidence condemned the accused person. As no one in the crowd can face up to Jesus' test of their sincerity the woman is left unharmed. Jesus forgives her, but warns her not to sin again.

8.   The Good Shepherd
John 10:1–18; 10:22–39

John 10:1–18 This is the only parable in John's Gospel. It uses the image of a shepherd being followed by his flock because they know him. The loyalty of the sheep is exchanged for the care and protection of the shepherd. Jesus' flock is much greater than just those disciples who have followed him from Galilee and Judea. To protect his sheep Jesus will have to lose his life. He will, however, regain his life and so be able to gather together the whole flock. Many could not understand because they were blind to the truth.

John 10:22–39 This story has the form of an unofficial trial to decide whether Jesus is the Christ or is committing blasphemy. It takes place in Jerusalem during the Feast of Dedication which celebrated the rededication of the Temple in 164 B.C. by Judas Maccabaeus. The Jews who demand that Jesus claim openly that he is the Messiah do not belong to his flock. They cannot recognise the shepherd. They are not seeking guidance from Jesus but evidence against him. He tells them that the works which he does in God's name are evidence of whom he is. The story ends with the Jews trying to stone Jesus for blasphemy, then attempting to arrest him, but he escapes.

9. Visits to Jerusalem

In John's Gospel Jesus makes five visits to Jerusalem. These are usually made during festivals when many Jews would go to worship in the Temple. In Jerusalem he argues with the Jews and they try to arrest or stone him. Several different stories are linked together during each of these visits. In the Synoptic Gospels the only visit to Jerusalem made by Jesus during his ministry is at the end of his life.

First visit:	(Jhn 2:13–25)	The Cleansing of the Temple and the prediction of the Resurrection, during the feast of the Passover.
	(Jhn 3:1–21)	The meeting with Nicodemus.
Second visit:	(Jhn 5:1–18)	The healing of the cripple during a feast.
	(Jhn 5:19–47)	Teaching on authority.
Third visit:	(Jhn 7:1–52)	Teaching during the Feast of Tabernacles.
	(Jhn 8:1–11)	The woman taken in adultery.
	(Jhn 8:12–59)	Teaching on authority.
	(Jhn 9:1–41)	The healing of the man born blind.
Fourth visit:	(Jhn 10:22–39)	Teaching during the Feast of Dedication.
Fifth visit:	(Jhn 13:1–19:37)	The events leading up to the Crucifixion during the Feast of the Passover.

10. Miracles

There are only seven miracles in John's Gospel. These are called 'signs' since they point to God who enables Jesus to work the miracle. The two miracles which are also found in the Synoptic Gospels are the feeding of the five thousand, and the walking on the water. The healing of the official's son at Cana may be a version of the centurion's servant which is in Matthew and Luke. There are no exorcisms in John's Gospel. The signs reveal Jesus' glory. However, if faith is based on them as spectacular events, then the faith is useless. They are symbols or acted illustrations of the teaching. The following list gives the sign and its importance.

The wedding at Cana: (Jhn 2:1–11)	Jesus is the source of grace and truth, through whom lives are changed.
The official's son at Cana: (Jhn 4:46–54)	Jesus is the source of life.
The cripple in Jerusalem: (Jhn 5:2–18)	Jesus shares God's work.
The feeding of the five thousand: (Jhn 6:1–15)	Jesus is the bread of life.
The walking on the water: (Jhn 6:16–21)	Jesus will save all who have faith.
The healing of the man born blind: (Jhn 9:1–41)	Jesus is the light.
The raising of Lazarus: (Jhn 11:1–44)	Jesus is the source of life.

For further information see Chapter Nine.

11. The farewell teaching
John 14–17

In the account of the Last Supper, Jesus gives a long speech to his disciples which ends with a prayer. The main ideas expressed are:

1. Jesus is the way, and the truth, and the life. (14:6)
2. Those who know Jesus will also know God. (14:7)
3. Jesus is in the Father and the Father is in Jesus. (14:11)
4. Everyone who believes in Jesus will do the same works as him. (14:12)
5. Those who love Jesus will keep his commandments. (14:15)
6. The Spirit will be given to those who believe in Jesus. (14:16)
7. Jesus and the Father will be in anyone who loves Jesus. (14:23)
8. Jesus is the true vine and the disciples are branches. (15:5)
9. The disciples must love each other as Jesus loved them. (15:12)
10. Jesus will die for the disciples, they are his friends and not his servants. (15:13)
11. The disciples will suffer as Jesus suffered. (15:18)
12. The Spirit will teach them and lead them in place of Jesus. (16:13)
13. The disciples will experience sorrow at Jesus' death but joy at his resurrection, as a woman experiences pain and happiness in giving birth. (16:21)
14. Eternal life comes from knowing Jesus and therefore knowing God. (17:3)

15. The disciples, like Jesus, do not belong to this world. (17:16)
16. Those who believe in Jesus and God because they hear the message of the disciples are one with Jesus and God. (17:20)

12. The true vine
John 15:1–11

Jesus uses the image of the vine to describe the relationship between himself, God and his disciples. Jesus is the vine, ie. the plant or tree, on which the disciples are branches. God is the vine dresser who cares for the plant in order to harvest a good crop of grapes. Every branch is cared for to be fruitful, those which do not produce fruit are pruned so that the fruitful branches will be more successful. The disciples have been prepared by Jesus' teaching but unless they maintain their faith in him they will be unable to bear fruit. They will then be cut off and burnt. Thus the disciples must keep Jesus' commandments and remain in his love if they are to continue as disciples.

13. The Holy Spirit
John 14:15–17, 25–26; 15:26–27; 16:7–15

The Holy Spirit is called the 'Paraclete' which can be translated as 'comforter' or 'helper'. The Revised Standard Version of the Bible has 'Counsellor' and the New English Bible has 'Advocate'. The Spirit will take the place of Christ in the lives of his disciples after the resurrection. It will teach and lead them. It is the source of truth which only the disciples will recognise. The Spirit will continue to teach those things which Jesus did not have time to teach. The despair of the disciples when Jesus leaves them will be balanced by the gift of the Spirit.

This understanding of the Spirit means that those who believe in Jesus have the ability to develop and adapt his teaching to meet new situations.

14. Love
John 13:34–35; 15:9–17

The teaching 'Love one another' is not a more restricted version of the Synoptic 'Love your neighbour'. This love is evidence of love for God and is the result of God's love for man. The disciples are not to be a closed community who will care for each other and ignore the needs of everyone else. They are an expanding group whose example of love will attract others. Jesus has chosen them to be his friends, not his servants. The servant will obey his master's commands because it is his duty. The friends obey the commandments because he understands their importance.

Work Section

Section A

1. How do we know that John the disciple is not the author of the Gospel?
2. Where and when was John's Gospel written?
3. Why may the Gospel have been written for exiled Jews?
4. How are people saved according to the Gospel?
5. How is John's Gospel different from the Synoptics?
6. Give three symbols used in the Gospel.
7. Why is John's Gospel called 'the Fourth Gospel'?
8. To which Jewish group did Nicodemus belong?
9. Which teaching of Jesus does Nicodemus find difficulty in understanding?
10. Why was the woman at Jacob's well surprised when Jesus asked her for a drink?
11. What did the water represent?
12. Why did the woman decide that Jesus was a prophet?
13. Where did the Samaritans worship?
14. How will people worship the Father?
15. What did the Samaritans believe about Jesus?
16. What do the Son and the Father both do?
17. How is Jesus uniquely God's Son?
18. What does 'Moses and the Scriptures' mean?
19. What was the Feast of Tabernacles?
20. Why did people wonder if the authorities had decided that Jesus was the Messiah?
21. Why was the Messiah expected to come from Bethlehem?
22. How do the Jews judge?
23. How many witnesses did the Jewish law require?
24. How is Jesus the 'Bread of Life'?
25. How can people eat the flesh of Jesus?
26. Why do some people understand the teaching of Jesus, but others do not?
27. What was the usual punishment for adultery?

28. Why did no-one condemn the woman?
29. How will Jesus gather his flock?
30. Why does Jesus refuse to tell the Jews clearly that he is the Messiah?
31. Which visit to Jerusalem is also found in the Synoptic Gospels?
32. What is John's name for miracles?
33. Which miracles are also in the Synoptic Gospels?
34. Which miracle stories in John's Gospel take place on the Sabbath?
35. How does the farewell speech end?
36. In the teaching of the true vine, what symbols are used for God, Jesus, and the Disciples?
37. What happens to the branches that do not bear fruit?
38. What does 'Paraclete' mean?
39. How will the Spirit replace Jesus?
40. What status do the disciples have?

Section B

41. What teaching does Jesus give about the Bread of Life? Why does this cause some of his followers to desert him? 14,6

42. What does Jesus tell the disciples about being the true vine? Describe the first sign which Jesus did at Cana. 8,12

43. What does Jesus teach about the Good Shepherd? Describe the washing of the disciples' feet. 10,10

44. Describe the occasion when Nicodemus went to Jesus by night. What does Jesus say about the reasons for God sending his Son into the world? 8,12

45. Describe the meeting between the Samaritan woman and Jesus by Jacob's well. What does it teach about the different customs of Jews and Samaritans? 14,6

Section C

46. Why do you think that some people did not want to include John's Gospel in the New Testament?

47. How do ideas like Light, Word, Truth, help our understanding of God?

48. What advantages and disadvantages are there in using symbolic language to talk about Jesus?

Glossary

Allegory:
A story in which every detail represents something else.

Christ:
The English form of the Greek word 'Christos' (anointed). It has the same meaning as 'Messiah' which is derived from a Hebrew word.

Day of Atonement:
(see Leviticus Ch. 16) On this special day each year a bullock was sacrificed on behalf of the High Priest, a ram for the priests, and a male goat for the people. The High Priest took the blood of the animals into the Holy of Holies and sprinkled it on the mercy seat. He then placed his hands on the head of a second goat and confessed all the sins of the people of Israel. This goat (the scape-goat) was then led into the wilderness. According to the Mishnah it was then thrown over a cliff.

Disciple:
One who learns.

Eucharist:
Originally Christians celebrated the Lord's Supper by sharing a whole meal together but gradually the sharing of bread and wine which Jesus had given special meaning to became separated and was called the Eucharist. It means 'thanksgiving'.

Exegesis:
The interpretation of the Bible.

Exorcism:
The casting out of evil spirits.

Gentile:
Someone who is not a Jew.

Gospel:
The original English word is 'God-spell' which means 'God-story'. It was used for the New Testament phrase, 'good news'.

Holy Spirit:
Spirit is a difficult word to define. It is connected with the idea of wind or breath. The The Holy Spirit is the link between man and God.

Kingdom of God:
God's rule over the whole world.

The Law:	This includes both the written law (The Torah) and the Oral Tradition, (see below).
Messiah:	In the time of Jesus the title Messiah was used for the King whom God would raise up to deliver his people from their enemies. Christians use it to refer to Jesus.
Miracle:	Something which happens in a different way to what is normally observed. In the Gospels the miracles are the signs of God's power.
Mishnah:	A written form of the oral law dating from the second century.
Oral Tradition:	(Halakah) This was composed by the scribes to apply the Torah to everyday life. Originally it was not written down.
Passover:	The greatest Jewish festival. It incorporates two ancient Spring Festivals, from one comes unleavened bread and bitter herbs, from the other comes the sacrifice of the first born of the flock (Exodus Ch. 12). After the exodus the Passover reminded the Jews of their deliverance from Egypt and covenant with God. In the time of Jesus people usually went to Jerusalem to celebrate the Passover. In the Synoptic Gospels the Last Supper was a Passover meal.
Proselyte:	A Gentile who had been converted to Judaism.
Rabbi:	A Jewish teacher, a scribe.
Righteousness:	In the New Testament the Greek word is used to mean doing the right thing and also the salvation which God offers.
Rituals:	Religious practices or customs.
Sabbath:	The day of complete rest from normal life which became a major part of Jewish belief.
Sacrifice:	This is derived from 'slaughter'. It was a gift to God which made up for disobeying him. Sacrifices were only made in the Temple.
Sadducees:	A powerful group of wealthy priests.
Samaritans:	The descendents of the Jews who lived in the Northern Kingdom (Israel) and married foreigners when Israel was invaded by the Assyrians. Samaria was between Judah and Galilee. They were the traditional enemies of the Jews even though their religion was similar to Judaism.

Sanhedrin:	The council made up of seventy Jewish leaders. It was in charge of religious life and consequently had power over everyday life.
Scholar:	Someone who has developed great knowledge and skill in an academic discipline. In this book it refers to an expert in the field of theology.
Scribe:	Someone who copied out the Law and so became an authority on interpreting the Law.
Sin:	The inability to do what God wants, either because the person is ignorant of God's will or because he has deliberately rejected it.
Sinner:	Strict Jews (Pharisees) thought that anyone who did not keep all the Jewish Law was a sinner.
Son of Man:	This usually meant only 'man' but it may also have been a title for the Messiah. It was the only title which Jesus used to refer to himself.
Suffering Servant:	In Isaiah 52:13–53:12 the servant suffers on behalf of others in order to fulfil his mission. Jesus suffered in the same way.
Symbol:	Something which represents something else. eg. in the Gospels the word 'Father' is used to represent God, bread and wine are used to represent the body and blood of Jesus.
Synagogue:	A Jewish place of worship.
Synoptic:	From the Greek words 'viewed-together'. The word is used when looking at the relationship between the Gospels.
Tax-collectors:	People despised by the strict Jews at the time of Jesus because they collected taxes for the Romans and were usually dishonest.
Temple:	This was in Jerusalem. At the time of Jesus it has been rebuilt by Herod the Great. It was very important for Jews because it was where sacrifices were offered.
Tithe:	Donating a tenth of earnings or crops etc. Jews donated tithes to the Temple.
Tradition:	In this book when tradition is used by itself it means a generally held belief or custom. 'Oral Tradition' is more specific, see above.

Torah: The first five books of our Old Testament which make up the written Jewish Law.

Biblical Index

'f' after a page reference, e.g. p79f, indicates that relevant information will be found on several pages beginning at page 79.

'f' after a verse reference, e.g. Mark 1:21f, indicates that information will also be found on the verses following.

Index

NOTES

NOTES